MW01146010

THE FLOSS

NOTES

including
- *Biography and Background*
- *List of Characters*
- *General Synopsis*
- *Chapter Summaries and Commentaries*
- *Character Analyses*
- *Critical Discussion*
- *Questions for Review*
- *Selected Bibliography*

by
William Holland

Cliffs Notes
INCORPORATED
LINCOLN, NEBRASKA 68501

Editor

Gary Carey, M.A.
University of Colorado

Consulting Editor

James L. Roberts, Ph.D.
Department of English
University of Nebraska

ISBN 0-8220-0834-3
© Copyright 1966
by
Cliffs Notes, Inc.
All Rights Reserved
Printed in U.S.A.

1999 Printing

The Cliffs Notes logo, the names "Cliffs" and "Cliffs Notes," and the black and yellow diagonal-stripe cover design are all registered trademarks belonging to Cliffs Notes, Inc., and may not be used in whole or in part without written permission.

Cliffs Notes, Inc.   Lincoln, Nebraska

CONTENTS

The Mill on the Floss

BIOGRAPHY AND BACKGROUND

George Eliot was the pseudonym of Mary Ann (later Marian) Evans. She was born in Warwickshire, England, in 1819, the third child of Robert Evans and his second wife, Christina. Her father managed an estate. She and her sister attended several boarding schools for girls. Miss Lewis, the principal of the second of these, which she attended from 1828 to 1832, had a great influence on her. It was here she adopted the religious devotion and self-repression which dominated her character up to the age of twenty.

Following the death of her mother and her sister's marriage in 1837 Mary Ann took charge of her father's household. With the help of visiting teachers she continued her studies of Italian, German, Greek, and Latin. In 1841 her brother Isaac married and took over their father's house. She and her father moved to a house near Coventry. As she had matured Mary Ann's religious beliefs had changed, and friends whom she met here further shook her faith in Christianity. She soon decided that she could no longer attend church in good faith. Her father refused to live with her on those terms, and she went to her brother for three weeks. A reconciliation was arranged by her brother and her friends, and she agreed to resume church attendance and returned to her father.

Her first published work dates from this period. It was a translation of Strauss' *Leben Jesu* ("The Life of Jesus"), which appeared anonymously in 1846. Also during this time, until the death of her father in 1849, Mary Ann contributed articles and reviews to a periodical edited by her friend Charles Bray.

She had found satisfaction in caring for her invalid father, but his death left her with a small income for life and no duties. For a time she traveled on the Continent and stayed several months in Switzerland. She returned to England in 1850, and soon after she became assistant editor of *The Westminster Review*. She became a close friend of the philosopher Herbert Spencer, and through him she met George Henry Lewes. Lewes was a professional drama critic and man of letters, actor, and author of a history of philosophy. He was unconventional, and his freedom of manners was shocking to some people. When Mary Ann Evans met him, Lewes was married but separated from his wife. Despite his marriage their friendship steadily deepened, and in 1854 she sailed with him to Germany. From that time they lived together as man and wife until his death in 1878. Their union at first made them social outcasts, but later they were accepted by their friends and society. Mary Ann's brother, however, severed all connections with her until, after Lewes' death. She married J. W. Cross in 1880.

Lewes' encouragement had much to do with Marian's new career as a writer of fiction, beginning with publication of three stories in *Blackwood's Magazine*. These were published together in 1858 as *Scenes of Clerical Life* under the pen name George Eliot. *Adam Bede* and *The Lifted Veil* followed in 1859, and in 1860 *The Mill on the Floss* was published. This was the first of Eliot's great novels. *Silas Marner* appeared the following year. *Middlemarch,* generally considered her masterpiece, was published in 1871-72.

From even a brief sketch of the life of Mary Ann Evans it becomes evident that there is a great deal of autobiography in *The Mill on the Floss*. The facts of the author's life do not match Maggie Tulliver's, but they are both the same kind of person. If anything, Mary Ann was a more intelligent and sensitive version of Maggie who was fortunately able to obtain a better education. Maggie's early religious views are an obvious reflection of Mary Ann's, and her particular affection for her father may be based on the author's life. In addition, a certain similarity is to be found between Tom Tulliver and Isaac Evans.

LIST OF CHARACTERS

Maggie Tulliver
The intelligent, emotionally sensitive daughter of a country mill-owner. Her life is the central story of the novel.

Tom Tulliver
Maggie's older brother, whom she loves in spite of his strictness with her.

Mr. Tulliver
Fiery owner of Dorlcote Mill. He is particularly attached to his daughter Maggie, whom he resembles in his generosity and emotional spontaneity.

Mrs. Tulliver
Mother of Tom and Maggie. She is the youngest of four Dodson sisters, and is a pleasant-looking, unintelligent woman concerned mainly with her household possessions.

Mrs. Glegg

Oldest of the Dodson sisters, and the one in whom the family's strict traditions are preserved in the purest state. She is cautious with money, unbending in personal relationships, and strict in observance of custom.

Mr. Glegg

A self-made businessman, now retired and concerned mainly with his garden and his reflections on the ways of women.

Mrs. Pullet

The second Dodson sister, a hypochrondriac married to a scrawny gentleman-farmer.

Mr. Pullet

The gentleman-farmer, whose character consists almost entirely of his memory for his wife's prescriptions and his affection for lozenges.

Mrs. Deane

The third Dodson sister. She was once considered to have made a poor marriage, but it appears to be turning out better than any of the others.

Mr. Deane

A shrewd businessman, new partner in the firm of Guest and Con., any.

Lucy Deane

Tom and Maggie's cousin. By Dodson standards she is the perfect child — beautiful, obedient, and always quiet.

Lawyer Wakem

Archenemy of Mr. Tulliver, who considers all lawyers to be in league with the devil. Wakem's legal skill is instrumental in ruining Mr. Tulliver.

Philip Wakem

Son of the lawyer. He has been deformed in a childhood accident and is highly sensitive about it. An artist of moderate talent, he falls in love with Maggie when they meet at the school Philip and Tom attend together.

Stephen Guest

Son of the principal partner of Guest and Company. He intends to marry Lucy Deane, but against his wishes falls in love with her cousin Maggie.

Bob Jakin
A lower-class childhood companion of Tom Tulliver. He becomes a peddler, and his glib tongue and shrewd business sense are an important aid to Tom's financial success.

Dr. Kenn
Anglican clergyman of the parish of St. Ogg's. He is a touchstone for the author's views on social morality.

Rev. Walter Stelling
A financially ambitious clergyman who is schoolmaster to Tom and Philip.

Mr. Riley
A local auctioneer who advises Mr. Tulliver to send Tom to school to Rev. Stelling.

Mr. Poulter
Tom's drillmaster at school.

Mr. Pivart
A new neighbor against whom Mr. Tulliver goes to law over water rights.

Luke
The miller who works for Mr. Tulliver.

Mrs. Moss
Mr. Tulliver's sister, who has made a poor marriage to an impoverished farmer.

GENERAL SYNOPSIS

Mr. Tulliver has decided to remove Tom from the academy where he presently studies and send him to a school where he can learn things that will raise him in the world. Mr. Tulliver has indefinite ideas on education, and he seeks advice from an acquaintance, Mr. Riley, whom he judges to be knowledgeable. Mr. Riley, although he has no definite opinions on the subject, recommends Rev. Stelling, the son-in-law of a business acquaintance, as a tutor.

Maggie eagerly awaits Tom's arrival. He comes with gifts for her, but when he finds that his rabbits have died because she neglected them, he repulses her. She retires heartbroken to the attic until Mr. Tulliver forces Tom to coax her down to tea.

Tom and Maggie's aunts and uncles — the Gleggs, Deanes, and Pullets — gather to discuss the boy's education, but Mr. Tulliver has already made up his mind. One result of his hasty decision is a violent quarrel with Mrs. Glegg, to whom he owes five hundred pounds. Tulliver fears that she will call her money in, and he determines to head off that possibility by paying it back at once. His sister's husband, Mr. Moss, has borrowed three hundred pounds from him, and Tulliver rides to see them to ask payment of the debt. But pity for that family's poverty overcomes him, and he lets the debt stand.

Meanwhile, Tom and Maggie with their cousin Lucy and their mother have gone to visit the Pullets. Tom becomes angry when Maggie upsets his cowslip wine and punishes her by paying no attention to her when he takes Lucy off to the pond. Maggie takes revenge by pushing Lucy into the mud. When Tom goes in to tell on her, Maggie runs off to live with the gypsies and be their queen. She finds some gypsies, but they are not what she expects, and she is very frightened before they return her to her father.

Mr. and Mrs. Glegg have been discussing the proposition of calling in her money from Mr. Tulliver. She is at last convinced that it will earn more where it is, and so she is receptive to Mrs. Pullet's suggestion (prompted by Mrs. Tulliver) that it would be best left alone. However, Mrs. Tulliver makes the mistake of telling her husband that Mrs. Pullet has interceded with Mrs. Glegg. He is so angry that he writes to Mrs. Glegg that he will pay in the money at once. To do this he finds it necessary to borrow five hundred pounds from a client of Lawyer Wakem.

Tom turns out to be the only pupil of Rev. Stelling, and he receives the full benefit of an education he does not want and cannot understand, an education consisting chiefly of Latin grammar and geometry. When he goes home at Christmas he learns that his father is about to go to law over water rights against a new neighbor, Mr. Pivart, a client of Wakem. He also learns that Philip Wakem will be his school-fellow after the holiday. On his return to school Tom quickly decides that Wakem is an inconsiderable person, a hunchback who is touchy about his deformity. However, he admires Philip's ability to draw and to tell stories of legendary heroes. During this term Maggie comes to visit Tom and grows friendly with Philip, whose cleverness she admires. Her presence, aided by an injury to Tom's foot, brings about a brief friendship between the two boys, but when Maggie leaves they quickly grow apart again.

It is two-and-a-half years later that Maggie comes to fetch Tom home with the news that their father has lost all his property in the lawsuit with Pivart. Mr. Tulliver has found that the mortgage on his property (taken out to repay Mrs. Glegg) has passed to Wakem. That news has caused him to fall insensible. His property is all to be sold, including Mrs. Tulliver's cherished possessions. The relatives agree to buy in a few things which the Tulliver's need. There is some thought that Mr. Deane's company might buy the mill and retain Mr. Tulliver as manager. Unfortunately, Mrs. Tulliver tries to insure this by smoothing things with Wakem. Her plan goes wrong as Wakem keeps the mill for himself and takes Mr. Tulliver on as a hireling. Tom successfully applies to Mr. Deane for a position with Guest and Company, but his father requires him to swear on the family Bible that he will take vengeance on Wakem.

Maggie's life falls into a round of housework and sewing. This is broken by a visit from Bob Jakin, who has become a packman. Bob brings her a gift of books. One of these turns out to be by Thomas à Kempis, and this book leads her to a life of renunciation of the world until on a walk near her home she meets Philip Wakem. Philip convinces Maggie that she must not give up her desires and offers himself as a friend and tutor.

While Maggie struggles within herself, Tom is at work in the business world. He saves his money to pay off his father's debts, and under Bob Jakin's guidance he goes into speculations of his own. He has just saved up enough money to pay the debts when he discovers that Maggie has been meeting Philip and that they have declared their love for one another. By threatening to tell their father he forces her to give up Philip.

Soon after this the debts are paid. On his first new day as an "honest man," Tulliver meets Wakem at the mill and falls on him with a stick. Maggie tries to hold her father back, but the excitement causes him to take to his bed, and he dies there.

Several years later Maggie visits her cousin Lucy and is introduced to Lucy's love, Stephen Guest. Lucy has invited Philip Wakem to join them, for he is a friend of Stephen's. Maggie finds it necessary to ask Tom's permission to meet Philip. Lucy guesses that there was something between Philip and Maggie and forces Maggie to tell her. She begins to lay plans to bring the two together again.

Tom meanwhile has been doing very well with Guest and Company, and he is offered a share in the business. He proposes that the company try again to buy the mill and make him manager. The outcome is left indefinite as he goes off on business.

A mutual attraction begins to develop between Stephen and Maggie, but both of them resist it. Philip quickly notices it but tries not to believe in it. Lucy never notices it at all; instead, she seizes on the mill as a way of bringing Philip and Maggie together. She gets Philip to maneuver his father into consenting to sell the mill and allowing Philip to marry Maggie. She imagines that Tom will be so pleased at regaining the mill that he will consent to the marriage. Tom will not.

Stephen, in a moment of weakness at a dance, kisses Maggie's arm, and she repulses him. She feels that this frees her, but when she goes to visit her aunt Moss, Stephen comes there seeking forgiveness. They declare their mutual love but determine to part out of respect for Lucy and Philip. But when Maggie returns, Philip becomes convinced that she and Stephen are in love. One morning Lucy goes out of town in order to leave Maggie alone with Philip. Philip was supposed to take the two girls rowing, but he sends Stephen in his place, so that Stephen and Maggie are alone together. Carried away by the current of their emotion, they row down the river past their stopping-point and go on so far that they could not get home before dark. Stephen convinces Maggie that she should go away and be married to him. But by morning Maggie realizes what she has done, and she leaves Stephen and returns home.

Word that she had been seen with Stephen at a town downriver has been brought by Bob Jakin, and when Maggie returns home Tom refuses to allow her in his house. Maggie and her mother take lodging with Bob Jakin, and Maggie finds work as a governess with Dr. Kenn, the clergyman of St. Ogg's. She is looked on as a fallen woman and cast our from local society. Eventually Dr. Kenn is forced to let her go because of persistent rumors that he intends to marry her.

A letter arrives from Stephen asking her to come to him. She is tempted, but resolves not to go. She plans instead to go away and find work. She is praying for guidance when the long-threatened flood breaks into Bob's riverside house. Maggie wakes the family, but in trying to get them into boats she is swept away in a boat by herself. She steers the boat to the mill and rescues Tom. They are going together to find Lucy when they are swept under by floating debris. Their bodies are found and buried together when the flood recedes.

SUMMARIES AND COMMENTARIES

BOOK ONE: BOY AND GIRL

CHAPTER 1

Summary

The novel opens with a description of the countryside around the town of St. Ogg's and the river Floss. Impersonal description quickly gives way to a more personal tone, and we see that the story is to be a personal reminiscence of a narrator whose character we do not yet know. The narrator notes a wagon passing the mill, and watches a little girl and her dog playing near the water. They remind the narrator of "one February afternoon many years ago" and Mr. and Mrs. Tulliver sitting by the fire in their parlor.

Commentary

Note the introductory images: the Floss hurries to meet the "loving tide" in an "impetuous embrace." This first sentence contains images which will be used and strengthened throughout the book. Note too how closely the activity of the river is connected with that of the land — "the distant ships seems to be lifting their masts and stretching their redbrown sails close among the branches of the spreading ash."

The little girl and her dog who appear here are a symbol, in the narrator's mind, of the story which is to follow, in which Maggie Tulliver is so often seen with her dog Yap.

CHAPTER 2

Summary

Mr. Tulliver states his intention of sending Tom to a different school, where he can learn to be "a sort o' engineer, or a surveyor, or an auctioneer and vallyer, like Riley, or one o' them smartish businesses as are all profits and no outlay...." Mrs. Tulliver wishes to call in the aunts and uncles to discuss the proposition. Mr. Tulliver says he will do as he pleases. His wife is shocked at his independence of his wealthier relatives, and Tulliver himself does not know quite where he should send Tom. He decides to ask advice from Mr. Riley, a man of some education. Mrs. Tulliver worries about how Tom will live, who will do his washing, and whether he will get enough to eat.

The talk turns to Maggie, who is said to take after her father. She is clever, but it "all runs to naughtiness." She cares little about her appearance and is forgetful in other ways.

This is all seen to be true as Maggie comes in late for tea with her hair in disarray. Mrs. Tulliver tries to persuade her to do her patchwork for her aunt Glegg, but Maggie expresses a strong dislike for both patchwork and her aunt. This amuses Mr. Tulliver. Mrs. Tulliver frets, because Maggie is so different from what she herself was as a child.

Commentary

Maggie Tulliver and her parents are strongly characterized at once, partly by their actions, but also partly by their speech. Mr. and Mrs. Tulliver speak a strong country dialect, but it never becomes obtrusive. Instead, it becomes a source of comic irony through contrast with the author's own vocabulary:

> "You may kill every fowl i' the yard, if you like, Bessy, but I shall ask neither aunt nor uncle what I'm to do wi' my own lad," said Mr. Tulliver defiantly.
>
> "Dear heart!" said Mrs. Tulliver, shocked at this sanguinary rhetoric....

Note that Maggie does not speak this dialect at all.

Both Maggie and her father are at once seen to be headstrong, inclined to have their own way against all objections. It is made clear that Maggie is not like her mother's family; in fact, she is considered "too 'cute for a woman." This is one of the main problems treated in the novel. We should note also her father's offhand reference to lawyers as "raskills." This attitude becomes highly important later on.

Mrs. Tulliver's nature contrasts strongly with these two. The author sums her up as "healthy, fair, plump, and dull-witted; in short, the flower of her family for beauty and amiability." This is exactly as she has appeared to be; and it is ironic because her family really does consider fair dull-wittedness to be the height of womanly charm.

Although he does not appear directly, Maggie's brother Tom is also introduced. He is said to take after Mrs. Tulliver's family. This is put in a humorous way, but it should be remembered as the story progresses. The standards of his mother's family guide most of Tom's actions.

The nature of Mrs. Tulliver's family traits are well portrayed in her speech and actions. She is supremely concerned with her household goods, with their maintenance and correct use. "Correctness" is valued above comfort. Correctness extends even to, or especially to, dying. The best sheets are to be saved for a funeral, rather than special use for the living. Notice also the images which appear in Mrs. Tulliver's speech and which are connected with her — food, housewares, keys, and storerooms. These, particularly keys, later are even more closely connected with her sisters.

CHAPTER 3

Summary

Mr. Riley comes to visit, and before supper Mr. Tulliver asks his advice about a school for Tom. He hints that he thinks it best to start Tom in another field, "as he may make a nest for himself, an' not want to push me out o' mine." Maggie is in the room, and she leaps to Tom's defense. She drops the book she has been reading, and Mr. Riley picks it up. It is *The History of the Devil*. Riley is surprised that she reads such things, but Mr. Tulliver says he didn't know what it was; he had bought it for the cover. Maggie shows off the breadth of her knowledge, but when she talks of the devil her father sends her from the room. He remarks that, unlike her mother, she is a little too intelligent for a woman.

Mr. Riley easily agrees that a good education is the best thing for Tom, and he recommends as a tutor the son-in-law of a business acquaintance. He actually knows very little of the man, a clergyman named Rev. Walter Stelling; but he has heard him well spoken of. Tulliver is anxious about the price, which Riley thinks likely to be rather high. However, he says Stelling is "not a grasping man," and he might do it for a hundred pounds, which is less than most clergymen would charge. Mrs. Tulliver worries aloud as to whether Tom will get enough to eat, but Riley assures her that Mrs. Stelling is an excellent housekeeper. Tulliver then wonders whether Tom would get the right kind of education, a good practical education, and not "the sort o' learning as lay mostly out o' sight." Riley is confident that Rev. Stelling can teach anything, just as a workman who knows his tools can make a door as well as a window. He even offers to contact Stelling for them.

The author observes that Riley is not giving his aid from any hope of gain, as the reader might think. He simply wants to be of help, and the fact that he knows nothing is no reason to refuse his aid by withholding his opinion.

Commentary

Emphasis is laid on Maggie's cleverness, and on her love for Tom. But others do not see her cleverness as she does—it is considered almost harmful.

Mr. Riley, though he appears nowhere else in the book, is fully characterized here as part of the background provided for the main characters. He is treated ironically, for the beliefs that are ascribed to him by the author are obviously not the author's own: "Thus, Mr. Riley, knowing no harm of Stelling to begin with, and wishing him well, so far as he had any wishes at all concerning him, had no sooner recommended him than he began to think with admiration of a man recommended on such high authority...." But in fact Riley knows no more of education than does Mr. Tulliver. The extent of his knowledge is that "Stelling was an Oxford man, and the Oxford men were always—no, no, it was the Cambridge men who were always good mathematicians."

Tulliver, on the other hand, is puzzled by the whole matter, and knows he is ignorant. But he is not shrewd enough to avoid joining Riley in judging Rev. Stelling on the basis of social standing. This situation is compared ironically with the books which Tulliver has bought, and which Maggie reads. Tulliver bought them because "they was all bound alike—it's a good binding, you see...." Maggie's knowledge of them, and their unsuitability for her, move him to remark that "it seems one mustn't judge by th' outside." Nevertheless, he does just that, as do nearly all the characters of the novel.

Mrs. Tulliver's excellence as a housewife is re-emphasized, as is her dull-wittedness. Mr. Tulliver remarks that he picked her " 'cause she was a bit weak, like"; and her own words show it—she expects no schoolmaster to have anything against Tom, who is "a nice fresh-skinned lad as anybody need wish to see." Note that, to Mrs. Tulliver, it is entirely fitting and proper to judge by the outside.

Her concern for her son is contrasted with her comments on Maggie in Chapter 2: "I don't like to fly i' the face o' Providence, but it seems hard as I should have but one gell, an' her so comical."

Alongside Mrs. Tulliver's particular love for her son we may place Mr. Tulliver's care for Maggie, which appears to be based partly on her cleverness, and partly on her tenderness of heart.

CHAPTER 4

Summary

Because Maggie is not allowed to go out to meet Tom on his arrival, she takes revenge by dousing her newly brushed hair in a basin of water and then goes to the attic to torment a doll she keeps as a fetish. Finally she tires of that and goes out to talk to Luke the miller. She tries to show off her cleverness to Luke, but he is not interested in any sort of learning. Luke reminds her that she has allowed Tom's rabbits to die through neglect, and Maggie is momentarily crushed. But Luke invites her to visit his wife, and she quickly forgets Tom. At Luke's home she is enchanted with a picture of the prodigal son, and she expresses her happiness that he was taken back by his father. She is pained by Luke's thought that the prodigal son was probably not much of a person.

Commentary

This chapter re-emphasizes things already seen in the earlier chapters — Maggie's impetuosity, her love for Tom, her mother's helplessness with her. At the same time, it introduces new aspects of these relationships. Maggie is seen to be forgetful even with persons she loves: she neglects the rabbits which Tom asked her to care for. And she is highly sensitive to criticism even when it is deserved.

Maggie's mother, however, is concerned with her daughter mainly as a reflection of herself: "Folk's 'ull think it's a judgment on me as I've got such a child — they'll think I've done summat wicked." This is the same attitude that Tom will take to her when they are grown up — that she is important mainly because her actions reflect on him.

Maggie's reaction to the prodigal son story is intended to show her tenderness of feeling, but it also looks forward to later events, when Tom, who has taken her father's place, refuses to take her back in spite of her repentance. Much of this chapter, including this incident, is seen from Maggie's point of view, and this begins to get the reader in the habit of seeing all actions in a way which is favorable to Maggie.

CHAPTER 5

Summary

Tom has brought home a gift for Maggie, a new fishline. He acquired it at some cost to himself, having had to fight every day at school because he wouldn't share the cost of toffee and gingerbread while he was saving the money. For this and for his promise to take Maggie fishing the next day Tom receives the admiration and gratitude he expects.

Next he proposes to go see to his rabbits. Maggie tries to head him off by offering to buy him some new ones, but she finally has to admit that she has let the others die. Tom reminds her of previous failings of this sort and tells her that he will not take her fishing after all. He is unmoved by her sobs.

After Tom leaves her alone, Maggie goes up in the attic to cry. She determines to stay there and starve herself and frighten everyone, but eventually her need of love and forgiveness overcomes her. She is starting down when Tom, who has been sent by their father, comes to fetch her. Their father correctly suspected that Tom had been hard on her. But once they are together the two quickly make up and share a bite of cake.

The next day Tom takes Maggie fishing, and he is pleased with her when she catches a large fish. This makes her happy and pleased with herself. She dreams that life may go on like this always, that they two will never change.

The narrator remarks that life did change for them, but that the thoughts of these first years were always part of them, and that the love of our early surroundings never fades.

Commentary

Tom is seen for the first time, but we are already somewhat familiar with him from what has been said of him. The author devotes a long paragraph to analysis of his character. He has the fresh-cheeked appearance which his mother loves, but the author tells us that under this appearance nature conceals "some of her most rigid, inflexible purposes, some of her most unmodifiable characters." This is essentially the way Tom will be throughout the book. Tom loves his sister, but insists she act correctly. He brings her a gift, but he will not forgive her for neglecting his rabbits until their father forces him to bring her down to tea. The author puts this directly: "he was very fond of his sister, and meant always to take care of her, make her his housekeeper, and punish her when she did wrong." This is part of the "correctness" which is his inheritance from the Dodsons, his mother's family. It is a sort of acquisitiveness, for, to Tom, Maggie is almost a possession.

In contrast, we are shown dramatically and are told directly that "the need of being loved" was "the strongest need in poor Maggie's nature." Tom loves her, but he has no understanding of her needs.

Another of Maggie's characteristics which is lacking in Tom is imagination. She imagines him so brave that he would save her if a lion were coming, but he can only reply that "the lion *isn't* coming."

The author takes the point of view of whatever character she wishes to concentrate on. But for characters other than Maggie, this internal view tends to be used ironically. This is true of Tom in this chapter: when he is angry with Maggie, he goes out "not intending to reprieve Maggie's punishment, which was no more than she deserved...why, he wouldn't have minded being punished himself, if he deserved it; but, then, he never *did* deserve it." There is an ironic contrast of Tom's thoughts as he sees them and as the author makes us see them.

Note the imagery connected with the river. Maggie thinks of the Floss when reading of "the river over which there is no bridge" — that is, death. And for the second time Mrs. Tulliver expresses a fear that Maggie has drowned. This is natural enough when living close to a river, but it also foreshadows the future.

CHAPTER 6

Summary

The aunts and uncles are to be invited to discuss Tom's education, and Mr. and Mrs. Tulliver are working out the details. Mr. Tulliver is not concerned about their opinions, and he cares less than does his wife about the money her relatives might leave to Maggie and Tom. Mrs. Tulliver laments that her children are so awkward with their aunts and uncles and wishes that they were more like their cousin Lucy. But she holds naughtiness to be more excusable in a boy than in Maggie.

Tom and Maggie meanwhile show their independence by escaping with a stock of the pastry being prepared for their visitors. Tom cuts the last cream puff exactly in half and gives Maggie the choice of halves. She tries to take the one Tom wouldn't want, but he makes her choose with her eyes closed. He finishes his piece first and becomes angry when she fails to offer him part of hers. He leaves her and goes off to join Bob Jakin along the river.

Bob is a poor boy who is knowledgeable in matters of rat-catching, tree-climbing, and such matters. He is bound for a rat-catching at a nearby barn. As they go along Bob idly tosses a halfpenny in the air and challenges Tom to call it. Tom correctly calls tails, but Bob covers the coin and keeps it. Tom, with help from his dog Yap, wrestles Bob into giving up the coin. Tom then lets it lie and refuses to go any farther with Bob, saying that he hates a cheat. Bob retaliates by throwing down the knife that Tom once gave him; but when Tom lets it lie, Bob picks it up again.

Commentary

The Dodson family traditions are the subject of a long comment by the author. There is a rule of correctness for every occasion, and emotion is strictly subordinated to it. Thus, "funerals were always conducted with peculiar propriety in the Dodson family...." The familial egoism which is described is the counterpart of the self-concern which will be shown by every individual member. It is also the source of their self-righteousness.

This is partly involved in the further contrast which we are shown between Tom and Maggie. When Tom divides the cream puff, he is scrupulously fair; but he is indignant when Maggie eats her part after he refuses it. "He was conscious of having acted very fairly, and thought she ought to have considered this, and made up to him for it." Just as later, Tom is not really hypocritical, but self-centered. Maggie thinks mainly of others.

Maggie is also contrasted to her cousin Lucy, who is a "good child." This is goodness by Dodson standards, and consists chiefly in being quiet and dull.

Bob Jakin's appearance here serves two purposes – it gives another example of Tom's capacity for self-righteousness, and it prepares for later development of the plot. Already Bob is a talkative creature, but he hardly seems the same person who shows so much cleverness later. This may be partly because we see so much of Tom and Maggie in the meantime, while Bob disappears until much later in the book. However, Bob already knows what is in his own interest, and he will not let false principle come before it.

Once again there is a reference to destruction by floods, preparing the reader to accept the sudden coming of the flood at the end.

CHAPTER 7

Summary

Mrs. Glegg is the first of the aunts to arrive. She passes the time by complaining how the old ways have altered, now that some of the family are later than others. She declines a bit of cheese cake because it is against her principles to eat between meals, but recommends that Mrs. Tulliver have dinner earlier and lectures her about providing so much for guests.

She is interrupted by Mrs. Pullet's arrival. Mrs. Pullet, a finely dressed woman, comes in sobbing. Mrs. Glegg is scornful when she discovers that her sister is crying for the death of someone who was no kin to them. Mr. Pullet defends his wife with details of the will the deceased woman left. Mrs. Pullet and Mrs. Tulliver go upstairs to compare bonnets until Mrs. Deane comes with Lucy. When Maggie comes in with Tom, she compares poorly with neat, pretty Lucy. Both she and Tom are awkward with their aunts and uncles, who talk about them as though they were inconsiderable creatures. Mrs. Pullet is of the opinion that Maggie's hair is too long.

Her aunt's criticism leads Maggie to decide to cut her hair off and be done with it. She gets Tom to come upstairs and help her. But when it is cut and Tom laughs at her, she realizes how foolish she looks and is mortified. For a long time she refuses to go down to dinner, but Tom at last coaxes her down. Everyone is properly shocked at her rashness, except her father, who takes her part. Mrs. Glegg proclaims that he is spoiling the child.

After dinner the children are sent out, and Mr. Tulliver states his intention to send Tom to Mr. Stelling for an education. It is received with general amazement, and with opposition from Mrs. Glegg. Mr. Tulliver says the expense will be a good investment. Mr. Deane remarks that Wakem the lawyer is also sending his son there, which Tulliver takes as a favorable sign. When her husband makes a jesting remark, Mrs. Glegg reminds him that his advice was not asked, and Tulliver answers angrily that she has been giving that herself. Mrs. Glegg in turn says that she has been ready enough at lending, a reminder that Tulliver owes her money. The quarrel quickly reaches a point at which Mrs. Glegg walks out.

The women soothe themselves by attending to the children, while Mr. Tulliver and Mr. Deane talk politics and business, and Mr. Pullet listens.

Commentary

The aunts and uncles are to be seen in relation to the comments on the Dodson family given in the last chapter. Mrs. Glegg is the strongest character among them; but her character consists entirely of rigid adherence to the Dodson code. She wears second-best clothes on weekdays no matter what the occasion, for "to look out on the week-day world from under a crisp and glossy front would be to introduce a most dream-like and unpleasant confusion between the sacred and the secular." "Correctness" is all, and she expects it in all her relatives as well as herself. She is as much oriented to *things* as Mrs. Tulliver is, but she always uses them correctly. And unlike Mrs. Pullet, she always maintains the correct social position — she cries for the death of no one who is not a relative.

Mr. Glegg is a sympathetic character whose words are usually intended to soften for some other character the blow of his wife's harsh judgments. Mr. Pullet is more narrowly characterized, but serves a comic purpose adequately, simply through repeated exposure of his narrowness. In this company the Deanes make hardly any impression except through the things other characters say of them. This may be in order to give adequate distance to them as "rich relatives."

The lives of these characters center on money and the proper disposition of it. Money is to be nurtured and correctly divided among one's kin on one's death. To die without having made a will is shocking. Money is not to be wasted under any conditions; it is best to die leaving more than one was believed to have. This will earn one respect and love — preferably at one's funeral.

Money is partly the root of the quarrel between Tulliver and Mrs. Glegg, but it is mainly a result of the clash of her instinct for correctness with his impetuosity. There are three passages preparing for the outcome of this quarrel: in one Mrs. Glegg notes that Tulliver has spent his wife's fortune going to law and is likely to spend his own; in another the author remarks that Maggie remembered her father's kindness "when everyone else said that her father had done very ill by his children." The third is Mr. Glegg's ironic little ditty:

> When land is gone and money's spent,
> Then learning is most excellent.

Maggie's closeness to her father is emphasized not only by his special kindness to her, but by her act of impetuosity which matches his. The act of cutting off her hair is typical of her in that she acts without foreseeing any of the consequences and then repents too late.

CHAPTER 8

Summary

Mrs. Tulliver reminds her husband that it will be hard for him to find five hundred pounds to pay Mrs. Glegg. This convinces him that he can find it easily. But the only way he can think of to accomplish this is to demand payment of the three hundred pounds he has loaned to his brother-in-law Moss. Accordingly, he rides the next day to visit Moss, who is a farmer in the impoverished parish of Basset. Along the way Tulliver encourages himself by thinking how it will be for Moss's own good not to let him slide by any longer.

The Moss farm is tumble-down and decrepit. Tulliver is met by his sister, Gritty, and her many children. He addresses her formally, to keep his distance, and asks for her husband. He declines to come in, saying he must return home shortly. Mrs. Moss asks about Tom and wishes that she could see Maggie. Her praise of Maggie's cleverness softens Tulliver in spite of himself. To Tulliver's remark that her four girls are enough for one family, she replies that they have a brother apiece, who she hopes will love and remember them. Her wish that Tom will also be good to Maggie affects him even more strongly, for it reminds him that Mrs. Moss is his own sister.

Mr. Moss comes up, and the two men go into the garden to talk. Tulliver opens by observing how poorly Moss is caring for his wheat. Moss defends himself by saying that poor farmers have no money to spare for that, and this slight quarrel allows Tulliver to remind Moss of the money he has borrowed. He says he cannot leave the money out any longer, but must have it back. Moss says he will have to sell his place to do it. Tulliver tells him that he must do it any way he can, and leaves him. He refuses his sister's invitation to come in, and rides off with a curt good-by.

Tulliver has not ridden out of sight of the house before he stops his horse and sits thinking. He returns and finds that Mrs. Moss has been crying, and that her husband has gone back to the field. She offers to send for him, but Tulliver declines. He tells her that they may let the money go, and that he will send Maggie to see her. His sister gives tearful thanks, and sends with him a colored egg which she had prepared for Maggie. Tulliver rides home feeling that he has escaped a danger, and that somehow this will make Tom kinder to Maggie on some distant day.

Commentary

Note the contrast of Tulliver's financial position with Mrs. Glegg's. Where she has more than the world realizes, "he was held to be a much more substantial man than he really was." Note too that we are given here the first hint of an attitude that assumes major importance later—that poverty is wicked, or that misfortune indicates a lack of virtue. It is ironic that these are introduced by Tulliver's thoughts, since he himself later goes bankrupt. He "got up a due amount of irritation against Moss as a man without capital, who, if murrain and blight were abroad, was sure to have his share of them...." This implication is the subject of a direct statement a few lines later: Mrs. Moss "thought it was in the order of nature that people who were poorly off should be snubbed."

The case of Mrs. Moss is handled delicately. It is clearly implied that there is a certain sense of shame at her husband's poverty. But she is seen to be the first person, besides Maggie, in whom love is of primary importance. This is particularly clear in the statement that "Mrs. Moss had eight children, but could never overcome her regret that the twins had not lived" — this in spite of poverty. She is contrasted with the Dodson sisters, in whom correctness and custom overweigh all emotion.

Against this background, Tulliver's action in calling in his money from Moss looks cruel; but the cruelty makes his change of mind all the more creditable.

In the conversation between Tulliver and Mrs. Moss, the references to brothers caring for sisters should be noted. These are brought to a point in Tulliver's fear that "if he were hard upon his sister, it might somehow tend to make Tom hard upon Maggie at some distant day...."

The author makes good use of metaphor to make her characters believable. For example, the comparison of Mr. Tulliver's actions to snatching a single thread from a skein makes an apparently inconsistent course of events seem perfectly natural.

CHAPTER 9

Summary

While her father has gone to the Mosses, Maggie has gone with her mother and Tom and Lucy to visit the Pullets at Garum Firs. Maggie is uncomfortable in her good clothes, but Lucy is pretty and neat as ever. They have been dressed early, so the children pass the time by building card houses. Maggie is not good at it, and she becomes angry when Tom laughs. He retaliates by saying he likes Lucy better than her. In her agitation she upsets Tom's card house, which makes him very angry. He pays no attention to her apologies.

At Garum Firs they are met at the door by Aunt Pullet, who sends out an old doormat for them to wipe their feet on, so that the good one will not be soiled. Inside the house it is the same — the stair carpets are rolled up to avoid wear, and the polished steps are slippery. Mrs. Pullet offers to show Mrs. Tulliver her new bonnet, but first it is necessary to unlock the linen closet to get the key to the best room, where the bonnet is deposited. The children are taken along to keep them from touching things.

In the best room the furniture lies in white shrouds, and the bonnet is wrapped in many layers of paper. Mrs. Pullet is mournful at the possibility that Cousin Abbott may die, so that she will have to wear crape and not get any wear out of the bonnet.

Tom has been entertained by uncle Pullet, whom he considers a silly fellow, even though he is rich. When the women return, uncle Pullet suggests they have some sweet cakes. Maggie manages to crush hers underfoot. This makes her despair, for she has been looking forward to hearing Pullet's music box, and now she is afraid that the pleasure will be denied her. However, she gets Lucy to ask their uncle to play it, and after suitable delay he obliges.

Maggie is enchanted by music, and when it ends she runs to Tom to put her arms around him. In the process she upsets his cowslip wine, and he rightfully repels her. Mrs. Tulliver, foreseeing further misbehavior, suggests that the children go outdoors.

Mrs. Tulliver takes the opportunity to open conversation on sister Glegg, but she is sidetracked onto the subject of Mrs. Glegg's and Mrs. Pullet's health, and Mr. Pullet's excellent memory for the proper time to take medicines. However, Mrs. Pullet is finally prevailed upon to intercede with Mrs. Glegg to let Tulliver's debt stand. Mrs. Tulliver is convinced that this must be done because her husband will never humble himself. She is still unaware of his determination to pay the debt.

Commentary

The "having" character of the Dodsons is fully exposed, but the comedy which accompanies the exposure partly disguises the author's seriousness. At Garum Firs, "good" things are never used: "the very scraper had a deputy to do its dirty work." Possessions are locked away and the key is locked up in turn. The children are not left alone because "they'll be touching something if we leave 'em behind." Even Tom is compelled to boredom despite the abundance of animals, for he is denied the opportunity to throw stones at them. The narrowness of these lives is shown in the ironic profundity with which the author invests their considerations on the merits of full-crowned caps, and in Mr. Pullet's interest in a bit of gossip. Yet money overcomes all deficiencies; even Tom has learned that. "He had described uncle Pullet as a nincompoop, taking care at the same time to observe that he was a very 'rich fellow'." Possessions are felt to determine character: ownership of a music box "was a proof that Mr. Pullet's character was not of that entire nullity which might otherwise have been attributed to it." Following earlier implications comes this statement of Dodson principles: Mrs. Pullet "did not forget what was due to people of independent fortune."

Compared to them, Mrs. Moss's strength is in her ability to *live,* and not simply pile up earthly treasures. The comparison is meant to be kept in mind, for there is an implied contrast between Pullet and Moss in the reference to the fat toads owned by that gentleman farmer, while "toads who paid rent were naturally leaner."

Lucy and Maggie are continuously contrasted throughout the chapter. Lucy is neat, she is quiet, she is already successful with men (with Tom, now), she is the good child who always does what she is desired to do. Maggie is an impetuous, imaginative creature whose soul is ravished by music, who cannot help but offend these straitlaced, self-important people.

CHAPTER 10

Summary

The gathering is startled by the appearance of Lucy, covered with mud from head to toe. Her condition is the result of the attention Tom has paid to her while he has slighted Maggie. To punish Maggie, Tom has offered to take Lucy to see the pike in the pond at the end of the garden, even though they were supposed to stay on the paths. When Maggie comes along, he tells her to get away. This is too much for Maggie, and she takes out her resentment by pushing "poor little pink-and-white Lucy into the cow-trodden mud."

Tom decides that "justice clearly demanded that Maggie should be visited with the utmost punishment," and he goes to tell on her. Lucy runs along with him. Tom takes her in the kitchen and tells the maid that Maggie pushed Lucy in the mud. The maid asks how they came to be near the mud. Tom realizes that he will be incriminated, and he walks quietly away.

While Lucy is being cleaned off, Mrs. Tulliver goes to speak to her children. She finds Tom and sends him to fetch Maggie. Maggie cannot be found, and Mrs. Tulliver is instantly certain the girl has drowned in the pond. But Tom suggests that she may have gone home, and they set out to look for her.

Commentary

Maggie's imagination is again contrasted with Tom's factual approach to life. He sees things only as they are and has "a profound contempt for this nonsense of Maggie's." But despite his realistic outlook Tom never sees any wrong in his own actions — he thinks of "the injustice of some blame on his own conduct." This is not so much hypocrisy as simple blind egoism.

This egoism compares closely with that of Mrs. Tulliver, who sees all things only as they affect her, even the actions of her children. "As usual, the thought pressed upon her that people would think she had done something wicked to deserve her maternal troubles...."

Lucy's personality thus far consists mainly of her innocence and beauty. Although she becomes more complex later on, she remains essentially a foil for Maggie, a reference point for Maggie's actions and emotions. She is here epitomized in the phrase "poor little pink-and-white Lucy."

Note that when Maggie disappears, Mrs. Tulliver thinks at once that she has drowned. This fear that her children will be brought in "dead and drowned" someday runs throughout the book and is prophetic of the end.

CHAPTER 11

Summary

Maggie has not gone home, but has decided to run away to the gypsies. She has often been told she is like a gypsy, and she expects they will be glad to have her and respect her for her knowledge. She meets two tramps in the lane, and one of them begs a sixpence from her. After that she crosses the fields to avoid meeting strangers. She does not know where she is, but hopes to come to a common where she expects to find the gypsies. While walking down a wide lane she comes upon a small camp. There is only one tent, with two women and several children. Maggie is happy enough with her friendly reception, but she wishes they "had not been so dirty." Maggie tells them she has come to live with them and teach them "a great many things," and the two women question her about her family and her home.

Maggie soon tires and demands her tea, but she is very dissatisfied with the dry bread and bacon she is offered. She begins to feel lonely, and this increases to terror when two men arrive. They talk to the two women about Maggie, and one of them examines the contents of her pocket and keeps her silver thimble. Then they fall to eating the stew which has been cooking over the fire. The women try to coax Maggie to eat, but she cannot. She says she had better go home and come again another day. She wants to go alone, but one of the men insists on taking her on his donkey. Her fear becomes less, however, when she sees a sign pointing to St. Ogg's. Just as they reach a crossroad she sees her father coming on his horse. He pays the gypsy for returning Maggie and takes her up with him. "Mr.

Tulliver spoke his mind very strongly when he reached home that evening," and Maggie is never reproached for running away.

Commentary

Here Maggie's imagination and Tom's matter-of-factness are contrasted in another way. Maggie has a romantic view of gypsies, but Tom is closer to the truth in thinking that "gypsies were thieves, and got hardly anything to eat." Already Tom is much better prepared for the realities of the world. He does not need an experience like Maggie's to open his eyes.

In running away to the gypsies, Maggie is motivated mainly by desire for admiration, especially admiration of her cleverness. She is somewhat conceited about her learning, but has no very clear idea of how the world, and the gypsies, will receive her. Yet, when she sees her mistake, she goes further than necessary in repentance: she "sometimes thought that her conduct had been too wicked to be alluded to." She is the only character so far who has shown any tendency to self-blame.

CHAPTER 12

Summary

St. Ogg's is "one of those old, old towns which impress one as a continuation and outgrowth of nature." It is named for its patron saint, who was a boatman operating a ferry across the river Floss. It is said that one evening when the winds were high, a woman with a child wished to cross the river, but no one would take her. Ogg took pity on her and ferried her across. When she stepped ashore, "her rags were turned into robes of flowing white," and she blessed Ogg and his boat, so that when floods came he saved many lives. When he died, his boat parted its mooring and floated off to the sea, but ever after when the floods came, he could be seen at evening on the water with the Blessed Virgin in his boat.

The old days have been forgotten in St. Ogg's, which "had no eyes for the spirits that walked the streets." Faith is of no importance to anyone, ignorance is "received with all the honours in very good society," and respectability is passed down from one generation to the next.

This is the town in which the Gleggs live. Mr. Glegg is a retired wool merchant who now devotes himself to his garden and his meditations on "the 'contrairiness' of the female mind." His wife is his best example of contrariness. He chose her because she was handsome and thrifty, but somehow her stinginess does not complement his own. Mr. Glegg is "a lovable skinflint," but while his wife is also a skinflint, she is less lovable. However, he has convinced himself that "a little daily snapping and quarreling" is not objectionable.

Today he is silent at breakfast so that there will be no opportunity to quarrel, "but by-and-by it appeared that his silence would answer the purpose." She scorns him for allowing her to be insulted by Tulliver. He replies that, as he has said before, she is wrong to think of calling in her money, since it will be hard to get as much return on it elsewhere. She tends to agree with this, but continues the argument anyway until Mr. Glegg hints that he has provided for her after his death "beyond anything she could expect." At this Mrs. Glegg retires to her room, apparently still angry, to cherish the thought of being a "widow well left." When Mr. Glegg comes in after his gardening, she is quite cordial, and agrees that she should let Tulliver keep the five hundred a while longer.

Commentary

The story of Ogg the boatman, and the author's comments on it, carry a main theme of the novel. Particularly to be noted are the words of the Virgin: "Thou art blessed in that thou didst not question and wrangle with the heart's need, but wast smitten with pity, and didst straight way relieve the same." Note too the imagery, the symbolism of the boat floating down-river as the soul departs in death.

The author's comment is greatly concerned with the record of floods and destruction in the past. This prepares for the flood which ends the book. There are also two general comments which use the past to shed light on the inner nature of present characters. One of these is that in past generations "many honest citizens lost all their possessions for conscience' sake" —as, in a different context, Maggie is to do. The other shows self-interest like that which we have already seen, but on a grander scale—war is thought of as "a past golden age, when prices were high."

Mrs. Glegg is further developed. The author frequently shows things from Mrs. Glegg's point of view, but always ironically. Probably this is necessary in order to make her bearable. Mrs. Glegg is severely correct, egoistic, and money-centered. But the humor with which she is presented saves her. There are some perceptive small touches: for example, that she had a particular book—*Saints' Everlasting Rest*—which she "was accustomed to lay open before her" on special days.

Mr. Glegg is equally money-oriented, but he has none of his wife's severity. He is "a lovable skinflint." Part of the author's analysis of him is important later if we are to understand the actions of Mrs. Tulliver's family after Tulliver's bankruptcy: "his eyes would have watered with true feeling over the sale of a widow's furniture, which a five-pound note from his side-pocket would have prevented"; for "charity...had always presented itself to him as a contribution of small aids, not a neutralising of misfortune." This is exactly the sort of help offered the Tullivers after Mr. Tulliver's bankruptcy.

CHAPTER 13

Summary

"Owing to this new adjustment of Mrs. Glegg's thoughts," Mrs. Pullet finds it easy to convince her that the money should be left with Tulliver. Mrs. Glegg predicts a dim future for the Tulliver family, but she intends "to set an example in every respect."

Unfortunately, Mrs. Tulliver, through her "irrepressible hopefulness," has told her husband that "sister Pullet was gone to try and make everything up with sister Glegg, so that he needn't think about paying in the money." Tulliver immediately writes to Mrs. Glegg saying that he will have the money paid by the next month.

The letter convinces Mrs. Glegg that Tulliver's "state of mind, apparently, was too corrupt for her to contemplate it for a moment." Tulliver's promptness also leads him, against his resolve, to borrow the money from a client of his old enemy Wakem

Commentary

The chapter title refers to the metaphor noted in Chapter 8.

The essence of the Dodson correctness, and its orientation toward death, is clear in Mrs. Glegg's decision not to alter her will despite Tulliver's stupidity. "No one must be able to say of her when she was dead that she had not divided her money with perfect fairness among her own kin...."

A single paragraph at the end of the chapter is devoted to the source of the money with which Mr. Tulliver repays his debt, an item of great importance in the plot. This is typical of the author's technique. The plot develops skillfully, but briefly, while the concentration is on development of character analysis of the society.

30

BOOK TWO: SCHOOL-TIME

CHAPTER 1

Summary

Tom is Rev. Stelling's only pupil at King's Lorton, and he finds life difficult. He is good at games but a poor scholar, and now that he has no companions he feels lost. Furthermore, he cannot despise Rev. Stelling as he did Mr. Jacobs at the academy, for "if there were anything that was not thoroughly genuine about Mr. Stelling, it lay quite beyond Tom's power to detect it."

Mr. Stelling is an ambitious man, impressive in appearance and eloquence, but of no particular ability as a scholar or teacher. He lives well beyond his means, for "a clergyman who has such vigorous intentions naturally gets a little into debt at starting...."

Tom is treated as a member of the family, but he has not capacity for Latin grammar and no comprehension of Mr. Stelling's sense of humor. Mr. Stelling has assured Mr. Tulliver that Tom will learn "to be a man who will make his way in the world"; but Tulliver has no definite idea of what is required, and Stelling knows only one way to educate a young man. Consequently, Tom receives a thorough drilling in Latin grammar and geometry, and Mr. Stelling "very soon set down poor Tom as a thoroughly stupid lad."

Tom is aware that he appears "uncouth and stupid," but he is unable to take any interest in his lessons. He longs for home, and to do something useful he watches over Stelling's infant daughter. He begins to yearn to have Maggie with him.

In October Maggie comes to visit. She is extremely interested in Tom's lessons. Tom tells her that girls can't learn Latin, but she shows a quick grasp of the examples in his book. However, she thinks his geometry is nonsense.

After she has been there a fortnight, Maggie begins to understand Euclid, and at last she asks Mr. Stelling if she couldn't learn to do Tom's lessons as well as he. Tom is indignant, and Mr. Stelling agrees with him that women "have a great deal of superficial cleverness; but they couldn't go far into anything." Maggie is crushed by this.

After Maggie leaves, Tom is lonely again; but at last the time comes for his Christmas holidays; and his delight in the homecoming makes it almost worth it, "even at the heavy price of the Latin Grammar...."

Commentary

Tom's school days cast light on his character as an adult. Note that like his parents, he cannot make out Mr. Stelling's true character. "If there were anything that was not thoroughly genuine about Mr. Stelling, it lay quite beyond Tom's power to detect it: it is only by a wide comparison of facts that the wisest full-grown man can distinguish well-rolled barrels from more supernal thunder." Tom lacks both the wide knowledge and the powers of comparison. Stelling thinks Tom is stupid, but this is unjust. The boy is only uninterested in Latin and geometry. It is made clear later that he is quick enough in other ways, and he has a good business mind. He would have been very quick at the sort of learning his father planned for him. But the education he receives has nothing of interest for his simple clear mind; it is aimed at the imaginative mind, and Tom is far wide of that mark. Maggie, however, enjoys this kind of learning

Stelling is a hollow person. His abilities do not match his ambitions, and the author tells us this with ironic humor: "he would by-and-by edit a Greek play, and invent several new readings." Stelling pays no attention to Tulliver's vague wishes for Tom, for "his duty was to teach the lad in the only right way—indeed, he knew no other." He has no conception of real scholarship, but a great willingness to bluff. But appearance alone is enough to fool Tom, and nearly everyone does.

The author devotes a good deal of space to the inequalities in education of the period. The only education available is not suited to Tom's needs. Maggie, of course, is in a more unfortunate position as an intelligent female person: her intelligence is either mistrusted or scorned.

CHAPTER 2

Summary

Despite Tom's delight in being home, this Christmas is not quite so happy as past ones. His father has a new quarrel going, and Tom is "distracted by a sense that there were rascally enemies in the world...." This argument is with Mr. Pivart, a new neighbor who is planning to irrigate his property farther up the river. Mr. Tulliver feels that this is "bound to be (on the principle that water was water), an infringement on Mr. Tulliver's legitimate share of water-power." Tulliver loudly assures Mr. and Mrs. Moss that this will be resisted. Mrs. Moss hopes that her brother will not "be forced to go to law." Tulliver does not know, but he is sure that Wakem is at the back of this matter.

Mrs. Moss tells Mrs. Tulliver that she is sorry to see her brother so "put out," and Mrs. Tulliver replies that she fears she will be driven "off her head" by his talk. Her constant warning is, "Well, Mr. Tulliver, do as you like; but whativer you do, don't go to law." But to Mr. Tulliver, any dissent by his wife represents all the Dodson females and only makes it more certain that he will do as he pleases. But even that does not "heighten his disposition towards" going to law so much as the thought of Wakem, the arch-lawyer.

The situation has not advanced by the time Tom is to return to school, but it has become known that Wakem's son will be sent to Mr. Stelling with Tom. Tom is uneasy, but "Mr. Tulliver in his heart was rather proud of the fact that his son was to have the same advantages as Wakem's...."

Commentary

Note the image used with the river: it "flowed and moaned like an unresting sorrow." Later it will become an image of the careless joy of love. Note also that once again music has a strong effect on Maggie's emotions.

Important plot matters are again given briefly in a few paragraphs. The background of the quarrel with Pivart is only slightly developed, while Tulliver's reaction to the situation is given first importance. There is a hint of things to come in Mrs. Moss's hope that Tulliver "won't be forced to go to law with him." This, and the fact that Wakem is Pivart's lawyer, begins preparation for the later sudden news that the suit was lost.

Tulliver is "a strictly honest man," but he shows again the bullheadedness attributed to him already, and a strong prejudice against lawyers in general and Wakem in particular. The clash of his impetuosity and his wife's caution is in a different way the same clash that occurs between Maggie and Tom. It is an expression of the conflict that occurs within both Maggie and Tom through their inheritance of Tulliver willfulness and Dodson correctness.

CHAPTER 3

Summary

When he returns to school, Tom meets Philip Wakem. Mr. Stelling introduces the two boys and then leaves them alone together. Philip is a small, deformed youth with a hump as the result of a childhood accident. Tom feels an aversion to him, and Philip is too proud and timid to speak, so they are both silent until Tom sees the pictures which Philip is drawing. He is struck with admiration for their realism. They begin to talk, and Philip says that he has taught himself drawing and that he likes Latin. He tells Tom that the Greeks were "great fighters," and Tom is eager to hear stories of heroes.

Wishing to even the balance, Tom tells Philip that he "thrashed all the fellows at Jacobs'" and allows himself to feel superior because Philip does not like fighting.

Commentary

Philip Wakem is a shock to Tom's sense of consistency. Although he cannot see that Philip's deformity is accidental and not inherited, Tom is forced to recognize Philip's superiority in other ways; and the fact that Philip loves his father gives at least a small shock to Tom's cherished prejudices.

Nevertheless, Tom has no desire to be like Philip in any way. He retains his disgust with deformity, and the things he is proudest of—his courage and athletic ability—are sufficiently different from Philip's tastes that they can never become friends. With his intelligence and sensitivity Philip is a good deal like Maggie.

CHAPTER 4

Summary

Despite his admiration for Philip's stories and drawing ability, Tom never quite overcomes the feeling that Philip is his enemy. Tom's schoolwork does not improve very much. Mr. Stelling is convinced that "a boy so stupid at signs and abstractions must be stupid at everything else," but Tom is not so very unlucky in his education; he is well fed, and gets "some fragments of more or less relevant knowledge." His bearing improves greatly through the instruction of his drillmaster, Mr. Poulter. Poulter is the village schoolmaster and a retired soldier, and his stories of combat under the Duke of Wellington are one of Tom's chief interests.

For a long time Tom has badgered Mr. Poulter to bring his sword to their drill. One day the old man gives in, and Tom runs in to bring Philip to see the exhibition of swordsmanship. Philip is singing at the piano and is annoyed by the interruption. He flares up at Tom, and in return Tom calls Philip's father a rogue. After Tom leaves, Philip cries bitterly. Mrs. Stelling tries half-heartedly to comfort him, but he tells her it is only a headache.

Tom is enthralled by the sword, and he bribes old Poulter to let him keep it under his bed. Tom smuggles it to his room and plans a surprise for Maggie when she comes to see him.

Commentary

Tom's lack of artistic ability is contrasted with Philip's skill. Partly this is the result of "a narrow tendency in [Tom's] mind to details," a characteristic we have already noted. This distinction between Tom on one hand and Philip and Maggie on the other, this tendency to details, is one factor in Tom's later success in business.

Much of the chapter is concerned, like the last, with the system of education under which Tom suffers. It is treated with typical irony. Stelling is compared to "an animal endowed with the power of boring a hole through a rock." He is "not quite competent," but "incompetent gentlemen must live." It is pointed out that "a method of education sanctioned by the long practice of our venerable ancestors was not to give way before the exceptional dullness of a boy who was merely living at the time then present."

But the author has more than comedy in mind here. These passages widen the social context of the story. They help to form a background against which the characters should be seen.

Mrs. Stelling is not a figure of any importance; she is a personification of a type, against whom other characters may be played. What is seen of her is not very attractive. She is a woman "who adjusted her waist and patted her curls with a preoccupied air when she inquired after your welfare." She is most important for what she lacks—"the power of love."

CHAPTER 5

Summary

Tom sees no reason not to make up this quarrel with Philip "as they had done many others, by behaving as if nothing had happened"; but Philip does not respond. However, when Maggie comes, she is interested in Philip, especially because she "had rather a tenderness for deformed things."

Tom has prepared a surprise for Maggie with his sword. He goes upstairs and then calls her up and appears before her made up with burnt cork and wearing the sword. He tries to look ferocious, but Maggie laughs. To better impress her, Tom draws the sword, but it is too heavy for him. It falls and wounds his foot.

Commentary

Tom has no conception of what might be important to others. Although he has insulted Philip's father, he "saw no reason why they should not make up this quarrel as they had so many others." Maggie is very different. She is open-minded, and "could not help looking with growing interest at the new schoolfellow." Furthermore, she has "a tenderness for deformed things." This is partly because they appreciate her petting, unlike Tom, who does not care that she loves him. This "tenderness for deformed things" colors her relationship with Philip even years later. It is always part of her love for him, and he fears with some reason that it is the only part which matters to her.

Nevertheless, it is a real love: Maggie is the opposite of Mrs. Stelling, for she does have "the power of love."

CHAPTER 6

Summary

Tom "bore his severe pain heroically," but he dares not ask whether he will be lame. Philip is the only one who anticipates this fear, and pity makes him forgive Tom. He learns from Mr. Stelling that the injury is not permanent and brings the good news to Tom. After this Philip spends his free time with Tom and Maggie. He tells Tom stories, and the one Tom likes best is "about a man who had a very bad wound in his foot, and cried out so dreadfully with the pain that his friends could bear with him no longer, but put him ashore...."

Once when they are alone in the library, Philip asks Maggie if she could love him if her were her brother. She answers that she could, because she would be sorry for him. When Philip blushes, Maggie feels her mistake. She says she wishes he *were* her brother. They promise not to forget one another. Maggie is struck by his fondness for her, and she kisses him, and promises to do so again whenever they meet.

When her father comes for Maggie, she tells him how much she loves Philip and says Tom does too. Tom admits that they are friends now, but he says they won't be once he leaves school. His father advises him to be good to Philip, who is "a poor crooked creatur," but not to get too close to him. But once Maggie leaves, and Tom's wound heals, the two boys grow apart once more.

Commentary

Philip, when Tom is wounded, is much more considerate of Tom's feelings than Tom has been of his. His own deformity makes him aware of

Tom's fear that he will be lame. Note too the story of Philocletes, which Philip says is "about a man who had a very bad wound in his foot, and cried out so dreadfully with the pain that his friends could bear with him no longer...." Philip has changed the story for Tom's benefit, for in the original Philocletes was put ashore because his wound stank. The change gives Tom a chance to restore his pride, for, as he observes, "I didn't roar out a bit, you know."

Maggie's pity for Philip is re-emphasized. She cares for him as she cares for Yap, who has a lump in his throat and is going to die. But she is also grateful that he cares for her. They are alike in valuing love of any sort.

Mr. Tulliver, in spite of his prejudice against lawyer Wakem, shows more feeling for Philip than Tom ever does. This compassion for people runs in the Tulliver family, and is seen most clearly in Mrs. Moss and Maggie. But none of it has passed to Tom.

CHAPTER 7

Summary

Tom goes on at King's Lorton until his fifth half-year, while Maggie is sent to a girls' boarding school with Lucy. She does meet Philip once on the street, but she is by then too much a young lady to honor her promise to kiss him. Once their father's lawsuit begins, even Maggie knows they are not likely to be friendly with Philip again. Tom brings home new books from school, and he is left with "a deposit of vague, fragmentary, ineffectual notions." Mr. Tulliver thinks it is "probably all right with Tom's education."

One November day Tom is told that Maggie has come to see him. She tells him that their father has lost the lawsuit and will have to sell everything he owns. "Tom had never dreamed that his father would 'fail'," and the news is "a violent shock." It is worse when Maggie tells him that Mr. Tulliver fell off his horse and has known no one but her ever since. Maggie begins to sob, but Tom cannot do that.

Tom tells the Stellings good-bye, and he and Maggie set out for home, with "the golden gates of their childhood...forever closed behind them."

Commentary

Maggie grows "with a rapidity which her aunts considered highly reprehensible." The things which her aunts have considered reprehensible — for example, her "wildness" — have always been of this kind, and not really faults. This is one device the author uses to gain the reader's sympathy for Maggie.

A few lines are given to bringing the plot up to date. We find that "their father was actually engaged in the long-threatened lawsuit," and that Wakem was acting against him. This is a casual introduction to the main action, but with the preparation that has been made in earlier chapters it is sufficient. It has another purpose: it makes the result of the lawsuit come as a sudden shock to the reader, as it comes to Tom and Maggie. But there has been enough preparation that the outcome does not appear implausible.

The passage of time is also handled economically. It is expressed mainly by changes in Tom and Maggie. Tom brings home new books and shows "signs of acquirement"; he is about to begin to shave. Maggie is becoming tall. These touches carry the story into a new phase.

The loss of the lawsuit is the central event in determining Tom's character, although it is less important to Maggie. Tom has always pictured himself cutting a fine figure, and now he is forced to readjust his thinking. This takes the form of turning away from his father's characteristic of putting up a good front, turning to the caution of his mother's family with its insistence that one have more than one appears to have.

Tom and Maggie leave childhood behind them at this point. The author expresses it in an image of Adam and Eve being driven out of Eden, passing the golden gates and going forth "together into their new life of sorrow." Note that the image of Paradise is taken up again much later, with reference to the love of Stephen and Lucy. Lucy at that point is still very much the trusting child, and the use is not inconsistent.

BOOK THREE: THE DOWNFALL

CHAPTER 1

Summary

When he learns that the suit is lost, Tulliver casts about for some way to avoid looking like a ruined man. He hopes to find someone to buy the mill and take him on as a tenant. "The really vexatious business" is that he has given a bill of sale on his household goods in order to raise the money to pay Mrs. Glegg. He thinks now that it might be best for his wife to go to the Pullets and ask them to advance him that much money.

Tulliver rides to St. Ogg's to see his lawyer about selling the mill. The lawyer is out, but Tulliver finds a note waiting for him. On the way home he reads it and finds that the mortgage on his property has been transferred. A half-hour later he is found lying insensible by the roadside.

Maggie is the first person Mr. Tulliver asks for when he becomes partly conscious. When she comes to him he recognizes her but falls unconscious again, except for moments when he "seemed to have a sort of infantine satisfaction in Maggie's near presence—such satisfaction as a baby has when it is returned to the nurse's lap."

Mrs. Tulliver sends for her sisters, who see the case as "a judgment... fallen on Mr. Tulliver, which it would be an impiety to counteract by too much kindness." Mrs. Tulliver wants Tom to come and seems to think more of him than of her husband. Maggie sets out to bring him home.

On the way home Tom ventures that Wakem is responsible, and vows to make him "feel for it."

Commentary

This chapter is a slight flashback in time. The end of it brings us back to the end of the previous chapter.

Tulliver's ruin is partly the result of his rash actions, but it is also partly a result of his generosity. We find that he has paid debts for Riley, as well as having lent money to Moss. But the quick emotion which is the cause of his generosity is also the cause of his stroke. He reacts violently to the news that Wakem holds the mortgage on his property; but he is felled by an imaginary dragon, for Wakem holds no grudge against him, as we learn later.

The Dodsons never show quick emotion, nor ever any generosity. They see this as "a judgment...which it would be an impiety to counteract by too much kindness." Too much kindness is not a Dodson failing.

CHAPTER 2

Summary

When Tom and Maggie arrive home they find "a coarse, dingy man" in the parlor. Tom immediately realizes that this is the bailiff who has come to "sell them up." Maggie does not recognize him, but is afraid "lest this stranger might have something to do with a change in her father." She finds that Mr. Tulliver is quiet, so she and Tom go to look for their mother. They find her in the storeroom with her "best things." She is crying over her mark, "Elizabeth Dodson," on her tablecloths. Tom says his aunts would not let the things be sold, but Mrs. Tulliver says she has sent for them and they will buy for themselves only the things they want. She tells Tom he'll never have a penny, but it's not his "poor mother's fault." Tom

Tom says he will find "a situation" and get money for them. Mrs. Tulliver says she wouldn't mind so much "if we could ha' kept the things wi' my name on 'em."

Maggie reproaches her mother for talking so and for caring about anything but Mr. Tulliver. She goes to her place by her father's bed.

Commentary

This chapter carries a fine characterization of the Dodson mentality and its faults. The title states the case: Mrs. Tulliver's possessions have become her gods. (Teraphim were the household gods of the early Semitic peoples.) The storeroom is their sanctuary. They are "only unwrapped and brought out on special occasions," like relics at a religious festival.

Compared to her possessions, her marriage is a transitory thing. Her concern is not for her husband, but for her china and tablecloths. She says, "I shouldn't ha' minded so much if we could ha' kept the things wi' my name on 'em," forgetting that her name changed when she was married. Her things are an extension of herself, and like all Dodsons she is entirely self-concerned. Note that none of the relatives will buy any of Mrs. Tulliver's things to spare her the anguish of seeing them go to strangers. They will take only the few things they need. Similarly, Tom has always considered his father to be right "simply on the ground that he was Tom Tulliver's father." There is no emotion to be spared for anyone other than oneself.

The bailiff comes as the personification of bankruptcy. His presence makes it real. Compare Maggie's and Tom's reactions to him. Tom thinks of his own disgrace, but Maggie is filled with dread for her father. She has the pity which the others lack. On the other hand, Maggie is wrong to forget that some blame is really deserved; but hers is a shortcoming which is easier to forgive.

CHAPTER 3

Summary

The next day the aunts and uncles gather for consultation. Mrs. Tulliver, "with a confused impression that it was a great occasion, like a funeral," makes the house look its best. Mrs. Deane arrives first. Her husband, who is rising in the world, is away on business. She offers to send jelly for Mr. Tulliver if the doctor orders it. This reminds Mrs. Tulliver of her cut jelly glasses which must be sold. The Gleggs and Pullets come soon after. Mrs. Pullet is much interested in Tulliver's illness, but sister Glegg recalls her to the subject of the meeting—"for one to hear what the other 'ull do to save a sister and her children...." There is no sympathy for Mrs. Tulliver's desire to keep her "best things." It is felt that she should be content with the bare necessities. As none of the family personally covets Mrs. Tulliver's things, there is no need to try to keep them in the family. As for Mrs. Tulliver's plea that she has never asked them to do anything for her, Mrs. Glegg replies that she should have, for "how are you to be provided for, if your own family don't help you?" Mr. Pullet ventures that Mr. and Mrs. Moss should help, and notes that they are absent. This reminds Mrs. Glegg that Tom and Maggie are not there, and that someone should tell them "what they're come down to."

Mr. Glegg observes to Tom that now some good will have to come of his schooling. He repeats his ditty:

> When land is gone and money spent,
> Then learning is most excellent.

Mrs. Glegg tells Tom that he must work hard and be "humble and grateful to his aunts and uncles," and she includes Maggie in the remark.

Tom says that since it is a disgrace to the family for them to be sold up, it should be prevented. He proposes that any legacies to be left to him and Maggie be given now. Mr. Glegg admires the proposal, but Mrs. Glegg objects that she would have to alter her will and leave less behind when she dies. Then Mr. Glegg agrees that it is useless to save the furniture when the law debts remain. At last Maggie angrily demands why they interfere if they don't mean to help. Her mother is frightened by the outburst, and Tom is "vexed; it was no *use* to talk so."

Mrs. Moss comes in and goes at once to the children. She discloses that she has three hundred pounds of theirs and is incapable of repaying it without being "sold up" herself. This was unknown to the family, and they inquire for details. Mr. Glegg warns that if there is a note, the creditors will force payment. Tom objects that it would not be right for them to pay, for his father didn't wish it. He says his father has told him that the loan was not to be paid back. Uncle Glegg then says that the note must be made away with. Mrs. Tulliver would like to sell the note and save her things, but Tom asks his uncle to help him destroy it. They go into Mr. Tulliver's room to search for the note. Mrs. Moss vows that the debt will be paid as soon as it is possible.

Commentary

Mrs. Tulliver does not know how to prepare for the family meeting. Since her code has no standard of propriety for bankruptcies, she does not know how to act. She is helpless outside her traditions.

The actions of the relatives are best understood if we recall Mr. Glegg's conception of charity (Book I, Chapter 12). It is mirrored perfectly in Mrs. Deane's offer, "if the doctor orders jelly for Mr. Tulliver...I'll send it willingly." Similarly, they are willing to buy a few of Mrs. Tulliver's "best things," but "it isn't to be looked for as your own family should pay more for things nor they'll fetch." Yet they talk about how much they are doing at the same time that any real aid is refused. Mrs. Glegg insists that Maggie must "respect and love her aunts as have done so much for her, and saved their money to leave to their nephews and nieces." But she will not give any of that money now, when it is needed, for to do so would be to "leave two or three hundred less behind me when I die." This is outside the Dodson code, and is therefore not to be thought of. In light of this, it is ironic that she should proclaim: "If we aren't come together for one to hear what the other 'ull do to save a sister and her children from the parish, I shall go back." It is ironic, but it is not hypocrisy, for she really believes she is right. It is only right that failure should be punished. "It's right as somebody should talk to 'em, and let 'em know their condition...and make 'em feel as they've got to suffer for their father's faults."

Because they are so self-righteous, the aunts and uncles are not affronted, but only amazed, by Maggie's outburst, even though she speaks the truth in saying that her father is better than any of them because he would have helped them. This is truth, but not to a Dodson. To them it is a "mad outbreak." Mrs. Tulliver "did not see how life could go on after it."

Tom, as we would expect, is not shocked, but only vexed because "it was no *use* to talk so." He is already clear-sighted and business-like.

Mrs. Moss's reaction, by contrast, is one of pure pity. She will help all she can, but that is precious little. Pity is unable to pay its debts.

There is a good side to the rigid correctness of the Dodsons; it is because of it that Tom insists on honoring his father's commitment to clear up Moss's debt. But the code will not work by itself. It requires compassion to set it in motion, and this compassion has already been provided by Mr. Tulliver. If not for him, the code would surely have required — as Mrs. Tulliver wishes — that the note be paid away to save her things.

Some of this compassion is still to be seen in Mr. Glegg, and it is this which makes him an admirable person here.

CHAPTER 4

Summary

Maggie and Mrs. Moss go to Mr. Tulliver's bed while Tom and Mr. Glegg search for the note in Tulliver's old oak chest. They take out some papers, but the chest lid falls, and the sound rouses Mr. Tulliver. He asks sharply what is happening. He recognizes his sister and Maggie and asks about Mrs. Tulliver. He tells Tom to take care of them, and reminds him to repay the fifty pounds which Luke had invested in the mill. Tom asks about the note, and Tulliver tells him he "mustn't mind losing the money." He says the note is in the box. When Maggie brings Mrs. Tulliver in, he asks her forgiveness, but says "it's the fault o' the law — it's none o' mine." He insists Tom must "make Wakem smart." He begins to become excited, and says that Mrs. Tulliver's family will "make shift to pay everything...and yet leave you your furniture"; and that Tom's education will help him; and that Maggie will marry. He falls unconscious again.

When the doctor comes, he predicts ultimate recovery for Mr. Tulliver. But Tulliver's words leave Tom clear that the note must be destroyed and Luke's money paid.

Commentary

The close identification of Mrs. Moss and Maggie is shown by the way they both go at once to Mr. Tulliver on his bed. Throughout the book these two are closely connected in feeling.

Tulliver's last words before he falls unconscious again show that his affliction is a way of escaping from a situation too harsh for him. He predicts that everything will be all right, in effect — that Mrs. Tulliver's furniture will be saved, that Tom and Maggie will have no problems. His only realistic remark is that "it's a poor tale." He forgets that the furniture cannot be saved because of the bill of sale he has already given on it, and is unaware that Tom's education is useless.

CHAPTER 5

Summary

Tom goes to see his uncle Deane about a job. He has no definite plan, but he knows he does not "want to save money slowly and retire on a moderate fortune like his uncle Glegg," but to rise fast like his uncle Deane.

Mr. Deane is at the bank, and Tom waits until he finishes his business. Mr. Deane asks Tom whether he knows bookkeeping. Tom admits he does not; nor does he know much else of value to a businessman. Mr. Deane feels "a sort of repulsion" for Tom's acquirements in Latin, history, and geometry. He advises Tom that the way to get ahead is to start at the bottom and keep his eyes open. But he says one has to be "the right sort of material" for that, and Tom's education will be a hindrance. Tom promises that he can "soon forget it all." He says he would rather do what will be best in the end and asks if there is a position open in the warehouse or wharf. Mr. Deane says he will help Tom, but for no better reason than that Tom is his nephew, for "it remains to be seen whether you're good for anything." Tom is hurt but promises to be a credit to his uncle. He is dismissed without a promise of help, but with hope.

At home Maggie asks Tom what their uncle said, and Tom says that his education is good for nothing, that he needs to learn bookkeeping. Maggie wishes she knew bookkeeping so she could teach it to Tom. Tom, having "just come from being lectured," is angry and accuses Maggie of conceit. His harshness drives Maggie to tears.

Commentary

The Dodson side of Tom's character is shown in his refusal to resent his aunts' failure to help his family. He too feels that it is not their place to "give away their money plentifully to those who had not taken care of their own money." Moreover, he is confident that he will never deserve "just severity." This is the attitude which colors all his future relations with Maggie.

Tom at this point still expects his education to be of use to him, and he still has some hopes of being a "fine gentleman." The world's view of him is shown to be very different. He is said to have been brought up "to turn up his nose at his father's customers, and to be a fine gentleman — not much else...." As we have already seen, this is the exact truth. He has no conception of what will be necessary to achieve what he wants.

Mr. Deane provides this knowledge. He is contrasted with Mr. Riley: unlike that man, he will not give unfounded opinions on education. "He was not going to speak rashly of a raw material in which he had had no experience." He does know business. The author presents him as a typical hard-headed businessman, but avoids caricature.

The irony of Tom's situation is summed up in his earnest statement that his education will be no hindrance: "I shall soon forget it all."

To cover his disappointment, Tom is "justifiably severe" with Maggie. By his taking command, we see that Tom is becoming a man; but he is a disagreeable one. He cannot understand Maggie's unhappiness with people who "show their kindness by finding fault"—a precise statement of the Dodson character.

CHAPTER 6

Summary

The sale of household goods is finally over. Mrs. Tulliver's face "seemed aged ten years." That evening Tom has a visitor, a young man in dirty clothes who identifies himself as Bob Jakin. Bob shows the knife which Tom once gave him, and recalls that "there was niver nobody else gen me nothin'...." Tom asks if he can do anything for Bob, but Bob replies that he has come to repay a good turn.

Just then Maggie breaks in looking for her books. Uncle Glegg said he would buy them, but she can find only a few. Tom tells her only those few were bought.

Bob tells them that he has been working on a barge and that two weeks before he had happened to see a mill on fire and put it out. The owner gave him ten sovereigns, but that is more money than he needs. Therefore he will offer it to Tom. Tom thanks him but refuses, saying that the money is not enough to do him any good, but that Bob can use it better. Bob regretfully takes the money back, after Maggie promises that if they need help in the future, they will ask him.

Bob's departure is hastened by the entrance of Kezia, the maid, saying that tea is ready.

Commentary

Bob Jakin has not been seen since the early chapters of the book, and his new character here is not exactly what might have been expected of that youth. Despite the author's attempts to connect Bob with that rock-throwing boy with an interest in ferrets, the man seen here is far more aware of the world and of himself. Bob is of a lower class than Tom and Maggie, and he knows his place. His language is rude; he tugs at his forelock by way of salutation. The maid can rightly give him black looks, and it is not felt to be slighting that he is not invited to tea. Yet he is the one person who is generous to the Tullivers, even though he has little of his own. It will become clear later that Bob is the one person who strikes the mean between feeling and planning — between Tulliver emotion and Dodson shrewdness and caution.

CHAPTER 7

Summary

Mr. Tulliver slowly recovers, but he is unaware of the lapse of time and still imagines himself to be in the "first stage of his misfortunes," able to find a plan to save the mill. His wife and children hope that uncle Deane's company may buy the mill and carry on business, but "business caution" forbids bidding too high. Uncle Deane is clearly interested in the family, for he has brought Lucy to visit them and he has found Tom a place in the warehouse.

Mrs. Tulliver, to help matters along, decides that by speaking to Wakem she can make certain that Mr. Deane's company will be able to buy the mill. She believes he must be kindly disposed toward herself, "whom he knew to have been a Miss Dodson." Therefore she goes secretly to Wakem's office and informs him that she is not responsible for her husband's actions, that she herself has never abused Mr. Wakem, and that it would be kind of him not to buy the mill. She tells him that Guest and Company are thinking of buying it and keeping Mr. Tulliver as manager. Wakem suggests that he could buy the mill himself and employ Mr. Tulliver, but Mrs. Tulliver says her husband "could niver be got to do it." She reminds Wakem that their sons were at school together; but at that point she is shown out of the office.

Wakem has never intended to buy the mill, but now he begins to see advantages in it. Tulliver's railing has never bothered Wakem and he does not feel vindictive; but he thinks it would be pleasant to "see an enemy humiliated" by his benevolence. And there are other good reasons for purchasing the mill, "quite apart from any benevolent vengeance on the miller." It is a good business investment, and Mr. Tulliver would be an honest manager. In addition, Wakem has other sons besides Philip, and the mill might in the future "furnish a highly suitable position for a certain favourite lad whom he meant to bring on in the world."

Commentary

Note how once again actions which are central to the plot remain at the periphery of the story while the author concentrates on the social and personal relationships which develop from them. Tom's job is mentioned, but never studied, even though in this part of the book so many lives are changed by his becoming the breadwinner of the Tulliver family.

Mrs. Tulliver is characterized as a hen. The metaphor makes tangible the foolishness of her actions and triviality of her mind. She vastly overrates the effect that her family connections will have on Wakem—a part of the general overrating of the Dodson family by itself. Indeed, she talks of "bad luck i' marrying out o' my own family," as though she would have preferred to marry within it. As usual, her actions have an ironic result: Wakem is not persuaded to sell the mill, but to keep it. Her argument is not well-calculated to rouse Wakem's conscience. A point to notice is her calling up memories of Tom's school days with Philip: "…and my boy, as there isn't a nicer, handsomer, *straighter* boy nowhere, went to school with your son…."

Wakem has been seen entirely through Tulliver's eyes. He now appears, not as a wicked-hearted lawyer, but as a clever but respectable man. His wickedness is made light of in an ironic presentation of Tulliver's views on the matter: "On an *a priori* view of Wakem's aquiline nose, which offended Mr. Tulliver, there was not more rascality than in the shape of his stiff shirt-collar, though this too, along with his nose, might have become fraught with damnatory meaning when once the rascality was ascertained." Nevertheless, Wakem has a certain amount of "wickedness," since it is implied that the lad for whom he intends to buy the mill is his illegitimate son.

Tulliver has overrated his own importance as his wife does her family's, for Wakem holds no grudge against him. He considers Tulliver only as an easy opponent, "a hot-tempered fellow, who would always give you a handle against him."

Note that only caution and lack of imagination keep Mr. Glegg from helping the Tullivers: "the thing lay quite beyond his imagination; the good-natured man felt sincere pity for the Tulliver family, but his money was all locked up in excellent mortgages, and he could run no risk; that would be unfair to his own relatives." Prudence matters above all, and things which have not been done before are unthinkable. Money is to be piled up for distribution at death—and not before. Even though Mr. Glegg wants to be charitable, he cannot; for charity consists in small things, and he cannot imagine it otherwise: "he would buy Mrs. Tulliver a pound of tea now and then…and see her pleasure on being assured it was the best black." The author is saying that pity by itself is not enough when there is the possibility of acting. Bob Jakin is given as an example of pity which acts to relieve a need.

Notice should be taken of the author's comment that it is inherent in our lives that "men have to suffer for each other's sins...that even justice makes its victims...." This becomes a crucial point in Maggie's dilemma at the end of the book, when she must forsake her friends and family or the man she loves.

CHAPTER 8

Summary

The land and mill are sold to Wakem, who proposes that Tulliver be retained as manager. This is regarded as a reasonable proposition by the aunts and uncles, although Tom protests against it. But when the time comes that Tulliver is able to move out of his room, he still knows nothing of this. Tom and Maggie and Luke go to his room to prepare him for the shock of finding that he is bankrupt. Mr. Tulliver is still planning a way out, but Tom tells him that everything is settled "for the present." Luke tries to show sympathy by saying that Tulliver would have paid everybody if he could. Tulliver then realizes he is ruined. When he calms down, he wishes to know what has happened, and Tom tells him that everything is sold. When Mr. Tulliver comes downstairs, the bareness of the rooms brings the fact home to him. He receives Tom's assurance that Moss's note was burnt and leafs through the family Bible thinking of the old times. When his wife comes in lamenting her condition, he promises to make amends any way he can. Tom tries to silence his mother, but she tells Mr. Tulliver that Wakem owns the mill and that she wants him to give in and be Wakem's manager. Tulliver says the world has been "too many" for him and wearily agrees.

Commentary

The basic failure of the Dodsons is seen again to be their failure to consider the needs of individual men. Tulliver's hatred of Wakem is considered "but a feeling in Mr. Tulliver's mind, which, as neither aunts nor uncles shared it, was regarded as entirely unreasonable and childish." Tulliver's hatred is certainly unreasonable, but the consequences of it run far deeper than childishness. This his wife's relatives overlook. They still consider their own feelings. They do not wish to be embarrassed by "that too evident descent into pauperism which makes it annoying to respectable people to meet the degraded member of the family by the wayside." There are varieties of Dodsonism: Mr. Glegg and Mr. Deane are not so strict as Mrs. Glegg, but "they both of them thought Tulliver had done enough harm by his hot-tempered crotchets, and ought to put them out of the question when a livelihood was offered him." Theirs is a just opinion, but a hard one to impose on Tulliver. It only leads to further trouble with Wakem. Another variation of Dodsonism is Mrs. Tulliver's: she is totally self-concerned and does not bother to try to understand what it is all about. Her question is, "O dear, what *have* I done to deserve worse than other women?" Like Tom with Maggie, Mrs. Tulliver cannot and does not try to understand the depth of her husband's feelings.

CHAPTER 9

Summary

As Mr. Tulliver grows stronger, he must struggle with himself to keep his promise to work for Wakem. His wife's sisters remind him "what he was bound to do for poor Bessy's sake," and only "dread of needing their help" keeps him from disregarding their advice. His inability to do other work, and most of all his love of his home ground, influence him to stay. But one evening his "choice of hardships" makes him particularly irritable, and when Tom comes home from work Mr. Tulliver tells him there is something he must write in the family Bible. Tulliver says he has decided to stay and serve Wakem, but he will not forgive him. Maggie argues that it is "wicked to curse and bear malice," but her father makes Tom write that he takes service under Wakem to make amends to his wife, but that he wishes "evil may befall him." After Tom reads it over, Tulliver has him write that Tom himself will "make him and his feel it," when the chance comes. Over Maggie's protest, Tom writes and signs it.

Commentary

Tom has become the man of the house. He is accepted as such by both his parents and by Maggie. This reversal of roles by Tom and his father is like that between Maggie and her father when she nursed him as he lay unconscious.

Tulliver's action in writing his hatred in the Bible is explained by the author in the next chapter. Religion is one thing and daily life another. This has been touched upon several times, and will be repeated when Maggie returns from her elopement with Stephen. Another aspect of his action, however, is that the Bible is the repository of family covenants, and Tulliver intends this inscription to bind his son. He has transferred all his hopes and desires to his son. This symbolic act has great bearing on Tom's later attitude to Maggie and Philip. He uses it to break up their early romance, and the fact that she disregards it causes him to distrust her.

BOOK FOUR: THE VALLEY OF HUMILIATION

CHAPTER 1

Summary

The great ruined castles to be seen on a Rhine journey are contrasted by the author to the "angular skeletons of villages" on the Rhone, villages which lend a feeling that "human life...is a narrow, ugly, grovelling existence...." Family life on the Floss may strike the reader much the same way through its conventionality and "oppressive narrowness"; but it must be felt if the reader is to understand the lives of Tom and Maggie and other "young natures in many generations."

The religion of the Dodsons and Tullivers is "of a simple, semi-pagan kind." It consists of "whatever was customary and respectable." The Dodson character is "a proud, honest egoism" that dislikes anything which is against its own interest. It will not allow kin to "want bread, but only require them to eat it with bitter herbs." The Tulliver character is much the same, but with a dash of rashness and affection. Such were the traditional views of the Dodsons and Tullivers, and their society contains no modifying influences.

Since pagan ideas are freely held, it should be no surprise that Mr. Tulliver "recorded his vindictiveness on the fly-leaf of his Bible, [for] church was one thing and common-sense another."

Commentary

The chapter is devoted to analysis of the people and the society which have been presented. The author states her intentions plainly: she wishes to impart "this sense of oppressive narrowness" of their lives so that we may understand "how it acted on the lives of Tom and Maggie — how it has acted on young natures in many generations...."

The narrowness in these lives has been demonstrated, and we are now told how it came about. The specific situation is related to the social structure, and the whole is connected, through the narrator, to the world of the reader. The analysis gives a sense of intimacy with this society as deep as the intimacy with characters produced by the dramatic portions of the novel.

Some of the main points of the analysis are that religion had "no standard beyond hereditary custom"; "vices and virtues alike were phases of a proud, honest egoism"; that life was rigidly controlled by custom. Moral and religious principles are not distinguished from social convention. The summit of respectability is a proper death and a proper will: "To live respected, and have the proper bearers at your funeral, was an achievement of the ends of existence...." Nevertheless, theirs was "a wholesome pride in many respects," and there is a core of soundness in the Dodson strictness. This has been demonstrated once, for a Dodson would never fall into the misery of bankruptcy through rashness. It will be seen again later when Mrs. Glegg stands by Maggie in her disgrace.

At the center of the work is the clash of the Dodson and Tulliver elements of character, the prudent caution and the "richer blood, having elements of generous imprudence, warm affection, and hot-tempered rashness."

CHAPTER 2

Summary

Maggie, at thirteen, is old for her years but lacks Tom's self-command. Tom throws himself into his work, but Maggie has nothing to do. Mrs. Tulliver remains "bewildered in this empty life," but this is less painful to Maggie than her father's sullenness. She finds it incomprehensible that they never feel any joy.

Mr. Tulliver refuses to be "reconciled with his lot," but all of the family feel that his debts must be paid, although that seems "a deep pit to fill. Few visitors come now, for "there is a chill air surrounding those who are down in the world...."

Commentary

Tom's and Maggie's characters are effectively summed up in a few phrases. Maggie has at thirteen years of age an "entire want of...prudence and self-command," while these are the very things that make Tom "manly in the midst of his intellectual boyishness." These phrases show Tom and Maggie at one stage in their development, but they are consistent with what we see of them throughout the book. Tom's "clear prosaic eyes" are further contrasted with Maggie's "feeling or imagination."

Tom is forced into concentration on one thing — "ambitious resistance to misfortune." Later he continues in this even after the need is gone. His resistance is largely a result of the Dodson "proud, honest egoism," with pride perhaps the more important component. The same circumstances, however, make Maggie to feel "pitying love almost as an inspiration."

Once again the lives of a few characters are placed in a larger social context by the author and connected with the real world. The Tullivers have few visitors since they are down in the world, and the author reminds us that this does not happen only in novels.

Note the changing imagery of the river. Where in the last chapter it was at once a model of society and "an angry, destroying god," here it is "pitying love" which flows in a "strong tide." All of these metaphors will come to fruition in the final part of the novel.

CHAPTER 3

Summary

One afternoon in the spring Bob Jakin, carrying a pack and followed by a bull terrier, comes to the house. He has brought Maggie a gift of books, chosen mainly for their pictures, but with others comprised of print. Maggie thanks him, saying she hasn't many friends. Bob advises her to "hev a dog, [since] they're better friends nor any Christian." He says Mumps is good company and knows all his secrets, including his "big thumb." He explains that his broad thumb gives him the advantage of measuring out the yard goods he carries for sale. Bob cheerfully admits that this is cheating, but he only cheats those who want to cheat him.

Maggie's merriment soon dies out when Bob leaves. Her loneliness is deeper than ever; where she has always wanted more of everything, now there is nothing. She longs to go to some great man and tell him "how wretched and how clever" she is, so that she may be comforted. But she is always called back to the fact that her father's sadness is deeper than her own.

Maggie leafs through Bob's books. One is by Thomas à Kempis. She begins to read, and is thrilled by the words that promise that renunciation of the world's delights shall bring the death of "vain imaginations," of "inordinate love." Maggie clasps this as a means of conquest to be won entirely "within her own soul." She clutches at self-renunciation with "some exaggeration and wilfulness, some pride and impetuosity," just as she has taken up sewing to help the family finances in a way calculated to give the most "self-mortification," rather than quietly. But she is sincere, and from this time her "new inward life" may be seen in her face and in her actions. But her "graces of mind and body" only feed her father's gloom as he sees his daughter being "thrown away" in the "degradation of debt."

Commentary

Bob Jakin is cheating but generous. He is made to appear far better than the Dodsons, with their close honesty. "I niver cheat anybody as doesn't want to cheat me, Miss" — the author makes this excuse sufficient. Note the images connected with Bob. He is a "knight in armour," and it does appear that with him "the days of chivalry are not gone." His life has a different standard from that of the Dodsons and Tullivers. Despite his low social standing, he is a distinctly knightly person.

Maggie's loneliness emphasizes her yearning for life and society. She wants love, knowledge, enjoyment. We are told that "even at school she had often wished for books with *more* in them." We are reminded of the strong emotions which music rouses in her. Music is made almost an image for her imaginative faculty. "There was no music for her any more" — this is significant of the atrophy of her inner life which is overtaking her now. She feels "the need of some tender, demonstrative love," but also "she wants some key that would enable her to understand...the heavy weight that had fallen on her heart." Her wish to go to "some great man...and tell him how wretched and how clever she was" contains a clear perception of her character at this point. She wants recognition of her good qualities and sympathy for her emotions. She expects these to be clear to a perceptive person. But she reveals a certain amount of arrogance — for example, regarding Bob "with his easily satisfied ignorance." This is part of the reason for her renunciation of the world. In Thomas à Kempis she finds "insight, and strength and conquest, to be won by means entirely within her own soul." She is egoistic about her own cleverness and self-sufficiency. Renunciation becomes satisfaction for her.

Maggie's viewpoint is used enough that the reader is likely to take her part, but in this chapter the author sets the reader at a sufficient distance to understand the mistake she makes. First it is hinted that she shows too much self-concern: "she was as lonely...as if she had been the only girl in the civilized world of that day who had come out of her school-life with a soul untrained for inevitable struggles...." Then her feeling is put in perspective by the author's comment: "She had not perceived...the inmost truth of the old monk's outpourings, that renunciation remains sorrow, though a sorrow borne willingly." It is clear that Maggie's view is not the author's own, for we are told that she brings "exaggeration and wilfulness ...pride and impetuosity even into her self-renunciation." At last comes the ironic comment that even in abandonment of egoism we seek "the path of martyrdom and endurance, where the palm-branches grow, rather than the steep highway of tolerance, just allowance, and self-blame, where there are no leafy honours to be gathered and worn."

All of Maggie's yearnings and her renunciation are important to later developments. Her wish for love and for understanding are the driving force in her relationship with Philip. Her self-denial is a model of her later renunciation of Stephen, which is based on the belief that "love of thyself doth hurt thee more than anything in the world" and on repression of "inordinate love."

The emotional nature of Maggie's belief, even now, is betrayed by the image used — that à Kempis' words are to her "a strain of solemn music." Her emotional reactions are always associated with music. This occurs with Philip, and far more strongly with Stephen. Nevertheless, the passage from à Kempis is at the center of her final renunciation of Stephen, when she determines not to "inordinately love" herself.

BOOK FIVE: WHEAT AND TARES

CHAPTER 1

Summary

One day Philip comes to the mill with his father. Maggie hurries upstairs, for she does not want to meet Philip in the presence of their fathers, where it would be impossible for them to be friendly. Maggie would like to "say a few kind words to him," for she feels that he would appreciate her kindness.

Maggie is seventeen now and darkly beautiful. She has stood well the "involuntary and voluntary hardships of her lot." The one pleasure she allows herself is a daily walk. It is on such a walk to the Red Deeps, a wooded rise near her home, that she meets Philip. Philip admits that he has waited there on the chance of seeing her. When Maggie says she is glad he came, Philip shows her a picture of her which he has painted, a sketch "of real merit as a portrait." Maggie is pleased, but remarks that she "really *was* like a gypsy." When she asks if she is now like what Philip expected, he replies that she is much more beautiful.

Maggie tells Philip that she wishes they could be friends, but that everything is too changed. Philip sees her point, but says that while he would give up a great deal for his father, he would not give up a friendship in obedience to a wish that was not right. Maggie says she would give up anything rather than make her father's life harder, for he is "not at all happy." Philip replies that *he* is not happy either. When Maggie says she is happier since she gave up wishing, Philip answers that there are things "we *must* hunger after...." He says he could be content if he could see her sometimes. Maggie is inclined to think that such meetings might "help him to find contentment, as she had found it," and that this new interest would help "to vary the days." But along with the "sweet music" of the voice that says this comes another voice warning her that secrecy would be necessary, and that would make it wrong. At last she declines to say yes or no, but agrees to allow him to meet her there to receive her answer. She then lets herself linger awhile, and they talk of books and music. She refuses his offer of a book, and he tells her it is wrong to "starve your mind."

After Maggie leaves, Philip goes home feeling that if she could never love him, he will endure that for "the happiness of seeing her." It is obvious to him that Maggie does not think of him as someone to love, but she might someday, and if not, he still might help her by "persuading her out of her system of privation."

Commentary

From the first, Maggie's feeling toward Philip has been primarily pity. She thinks he might still "like her to look at him kindly." Later this becomes the key to the guilty feelings she has about him when she is attracted to Stephen. It is also the key to Philip's jealousy, for "there was bitterness to him in the perception that Maggie was almost as frank and unconstrained towards him as when she was a child."

Philip produces a mixed reaction in the reader. He is never made clearly pitiable. He displays a keen self-concern which is at times irritating. When Maggie says her father is not happy, he answers: "No more am I...*I* am not happy." And he begs her to "have some feeling for *me* as well as for others." Moreover, his proposal to meet Maggie in secret makes him appear untrustworthy. But there is reassurance in the passages given from his own point of view. He certainly intends to act for Maggie's benefit. There is also some uncertainty about the extent of Philip's abilities. We are told that his picture of Maggie was "of real merit," but his philosophizing about "the strongest effects of our natures" is not very convincing.

Maggie's character contains a good deal of adolescent sentimentality, including her "ardours of renunciation." She rejects Philip's friendship because "it would make me long to see and know many things—it would make me long for a full life." She is still the martyr to herself. But there are hints of sterner things in her, and of ideas which are developed later in the novel. One of these is self-sacrifice for others. Note how this is connected with music: "Yet the music would swell out again...persuading her...that there was such a thing as futile sacrifice for one to the injury of another."

Note too that music as a symbol for feeling and imagination is closely connected with both Maggie and Philip: it is a ground on which they meet.

CHAPTER 2

Summary

While Maggie has struggled "within her own soul," Tom has been "gaining more definite conquests." His salary has been raised, and it is hinted that he might be trusted to travel for the firm. All of Tom's money goes into his father's tin box; for despite his "very strong appetite for pleasure" he is shrewd enough to see that only "present abstinence" can gain that end. Now that Tom is doing well, the family begin to talk of doing something for the boy.

Bob Jakin visits Tom and Maggie regularly, and one evening he asks Tom privately if he would be interested in "sending out a bit of cargo to foreign ports." Bob has a ship-captain friend who is willing to help. All of Tom's money is in his father's care, and Mr. Tulliver cannot bear to part with any of it, for if it was lost he would never be able to make up the loss in his lifetime. He wants to accumulate enough to pay all the debts at once.

Tom is not willing to give up altogether, so he goes to Mr. Glegg. Bob goes along to explain the proposition. Bob's loquacity leaves Mr. Glegg astonished and amused, but he is interested and asks to hear more. Tom desires a small loan at interest. When Mr. Glegg asks what Bob gets from Tom, Bob first answers that he is doing it for friendship; but when he sees that Mr. Glegg does not approve, he adds that a bigger purchase makes him look big, and it's "money in [the] pocket in the end."

Mrs. Glegg calls her husband to tea, telling Bob that he needn't stay. Tom is to bring his business inside. Bob says that he knows his place, but that Mrs. Glegg might do well to deal with the packmen she scorns. However, he admits that times are not what they once were, and pack-goods are not of the old quality. All he has is "bargains picked up dirt cheap," with only a little damage that won't show — nothing he could offer her.

When Mrs. Glegg finds that Bob's speculation may pay large interest, she is offended at being left out, but she is equally offended at being asked to contribute. Mr. Glegg decides to let Tom have fifty pounds, and his wife is indignant that she is not asked a second time. Bob admires her business acumen, and wishes he had it so he wouldn't lose money on his pack. Mrs. Glegg becomes interested in his goods. Bob is unwilling to show a sample, but does so on her demand, all the while complaining that his things should be saved for poorer women, for "three times the money for a thing as isn't half so good" is nothing to a lady like her. He is at last persuaded to sell her two damaged pieces.

Mr. Glegg is setting out with Bob and Tom to finish their business with the captain when Mrs. Glegg calls them back, insisting that she is not finished speaking. She has decided to lend Tom twenty pounds of her own. She demands interest, as giving was "niver looked for" in her family.

Tom enters this speculation without telling his father, and when it pays off he expands his operations so that by the time of Maggie's meeting with Philip he has a hundred and fifty pounds of his own and expects to pay off the debts by the end of another year.

Commentary

Tom has the same appetite for pleasure that Maggie has, but with it he combines the Dodson self-control. "His practical shrewdness told him that the means to such achievements could only lie for him in present abstinence and self-denial...." He, like Maggie, practices self-denial but for an entirely different reason. The author tells us he is "a character at unity with itself," and it is true that he "has no visions beyond the distinctly possible."

But it is Bob Jakin who provides Tom the means of achieving his ambitions. Of all the characters in the novel, Bob is the one who does the most to move the world for his own ends. At the same time, he is one of the few fully generous persons to be found. His generosity and initiative are contrasted to the Gleggs' caution even in charity to their own nephew. They require security for their aid: Mr. Glegg wants to help Tom "some time, when an opportunity offered of doing so in a prudent manner, without ultimate loss...." Bob has initiative; his head is "all alive inside like an old cheese...."; but he is more shrewd than Mrs. Glegg herself.

The irony of this chapter arises from this contrast between Bob and Mrs. Glegg, set beside the fact that she considers herself better than him both morally and mentally—a supposition based entirely on her superior fortune. Bob perceives Mrs. Glegg's true nature, and his main sales-pitch is aimed at her private miserliness. He degrades his merchandise as "not fit to offer rich folks as can pay for the look o' things as nobody sees." He is so skillful that she remains patronizing even while she is being taken.

Mr. Tulliver's former generosity is changing to closeness. Because of his strong nature earlier, the change is all the more impressive. It is most powerfully expressed in his conversation with his son about their growing hoard of coin: "...I wouldn't pay a dividend with the first hundred, because I wanted to see it all in a lump—and when I see it, I'm sure on't." Circumstances force Tulliver to take on some of the Dodson caution; but his passionate nature still forces him to consider the world a personal adversary.

Note that this chapter is a flashback in time. The last paragraph occurs just before the time of Maggie's first meeting with Philip.

CHAPTER 3

Summary

Maggie goes home from the meeting with Philip thinking that further meetings would be a kindness to him and at the same time would make "her mind more worthy of its highest service...." Nevertheless, she feels a warning that she is throwing herself under the "guidance of illimitable wants." When they meet again, she says first that concealment is wrong and that discovery would bring misery. However, she agrees to stay another half-hour. Philip tells her he has started another picture of her and that he must study her now while he can. When Maggie remarks that he thinks more of painting than of anything, he replies that he thinks of too many things. He has "susceptibility in every direction, and effective faculty in none"; but unlike most men he is unsatisfied with mediocrity. Maggie says she once thought she could not bear life as it was always the same, but resignation has brought her peace. Philip tells her that "stupefaction is not resignation" and that she is trying to stupefy herself. Maggie feels the truth of this and yet feels that it is false to apply it to her conduct.

Philip wishes to talk of other things while they can be together, so Maggie asks him to sing. He sings a song familiar from their days together at King's Lorton. Maggie cannot bear the memory and starts to go. Philip tries again to convince her that she cannot carry on "this self-torture." She still refuses to stay; but she does not deny Philip the opportunity to come there again and meet her by chance. She is even happy at "this subterfuge."

Philip justifies this to himself by thinking that it will be "better for Maggie's future life"; but he is "half independent of justifying motives" because of his longing for Maggie. His deformity, and the fact that even Maggie feels only pity for him, only increase his need. He has never known a mother's love, and his "half-feminine...sensitiveness" causes a repulsion toward his father's worldliness, so that "this one strong natural tie...was like an aching limb to him." These also make his need greater, and his personal desire is as great as his good intentions.

Commentary

Philip is cleverly handled by the author. He is not an attractive character, but Maggie's relationship with him is made acceptable, and it is necessary to admit his superior understanding. "Resignation is the willing endurance of a pain that is not allayed," he says. This is exactly what the author has said with reference to Thomas à Kempis. Philip recognizes that Maggie's renunciation is self-delusive. He tries to do the right thing for her: his "sense of the situation was too complete for him not to be visited with glancing fears lest he had been intervening too presumptuously in the action of Maggie's conscience...." The author provides a direct comment to excuse his temptation of Maggie, saying that he is more strongly tempted because of his deformity. But this is part of the reason for the uneasiness he arouses; his deformity, his "half-feminine...sensitiveness," counterbalance his good intentions and make his clear understanding seem less important.

Maggie accepts Philip partly as a source of personal gratification: "here was an opportunity indicated for making her mind more worthy of its highest service...." However, they are clearly two people of the same mold. Both feel, "I never felt that I had enough music — I wanted more instruments playing together — I wanted voices to be fuller and deeper." Both of them hate to "always be doing things of no consequence, and never know anything greater." Few of the other characters are like this.

The relationship between Maggie and Philip which begins here is an early model for that between her and Stephen. She dislikes the need for secrecy, the misery which could arise from discovery. She intends to send him away. But she fails, for the same reason she fails with Stephen — she allows the possibility of accidental contact. This does not offend her conscience. "Then, after hours of clear reasoning and firm conviction, we snatch at any sophistry that will nullify our long struggles, and bring us the defeat that we love better than victory."

CHAPTER 4

Summary

It is April nearly a year later. Maggie is returning a book to Philip in the Red Deeps. She tells him she disliked the book because the fair-haired heroine once again won away all the love from the dark woman. She says she wants to avenge all the "dark unhappy ones." Philip tells her that perhaps she will do so by carrying away all the love from her cousin Lucy, who "is sure to have some handsome young man of St. Ogg's at her feet now."

Maggie does not like to have her nonsense applied to anything real, and she would never be Lucy's rival. She says she is not jealous for herself, but for "unhappy people," and she always takes the side of the "rejected lover." Philip asks if she would reject one herself, and when she playfully says she might if he were conceited, he asks her to suppose it were someone who "had nothing to be conceited about," who loved her and was happy to see her at rare moments.

Maggie, aware that he is declaring his love, falls silent. Philip asks her to forget what he has said, but she says that though she has never thought of him as a lover, she does love him. However, she asks that no more be said about it lest it "lead to evil." He tells her their love can overcome any obstacle and he reminds her of her long-ago promise to kiss him. She does so now; but Philip is still not content, for Maggie seems unhappy. She reminds him that she can never injure her father and that they can never be more than friends. As they part she fears she has unintentionally hurt Philip. She tells him she should like "never to part, [in] one of those dangerous moments when speech is at once sincere and deceptive," when feeling is at a height not reached again.

Commentary

Once again the relationship of Maggie and Philip contains something prophetic of later events. She says she is "determined to read no more books where the blond-haired women carry away all the happiness...I want to avenge...the dark unhappy ones." She is offended when Philip applies this to her cousin Lucy; but this becomes one of those instances when she later drifts into a situation which is contrary to her best resolutions because she lacks the foresight to consider practical results.

It is made clear that Maggie's love for Philip is real to her, but not permanent. "It was one of those dangerous moments...when feeling, rising high above its average depth, leaves flood-marks which are never reached again." (Note the river image.) This prepares for her later abandonment of Philip. Even now, there is something uncomfortable in the relationship. Maggie "stooped her tall head to kiss the pale face that was full of pleading, timid love—like a woman's." This reversal of roles appears almost unnatural, and the author later makes Stephen's masculine strength come as a relief.

CHAPTER 5

Summary

Maggie has always feared meeting Tom or her father while walking with Philip, but it has never occurred to her to worry about aunt Pullet.

Nevertheless, it is aunt Pullet who gives her away by remarking one day that she frequently sees Philip Wakem at the Red Deeps. She means only that she has twice seen Philip there, but Maggie blushes and Tom notices it. The next afternoon while Tom is talking to Bob Jakin on the wharf, Bob points out Philip on the far bank.

Tom hurries home and meets Maggie coming out the gate. When she asks why he is home, Tom says he has come to meet Philip with her. She says she will not go, but Tom insists that she will. He threatens to tell their father unless she tell "everything that has passed" between her and Philip. She says she will tell it for her father's sake. Tom is scornful at that, but he forces out of her the fact that she and Philip have declared their love. Tom tells her she must either swear on the Bible not to meet Philip again or he will tell their father everything. He asks why he should work to pay their father's debts if she is to "bring madness and vexation on him" just when he "might hold up his head once more." Maggie feels sudden joy at this hint that the debts are to be paid; she begins to blame herself and tells Tom she was lonely and sorry for Philip and that she thinks "enmity and hatred are wicked." She says she must see Philip once more, and Tom says he will go with her after she swears her oath.

Maggie hopes Philip will not be there but he is. Tom accuses him of taking advantage of "a young girl's foolishness." Philip retorts that he honors her more than Tom does and says Tom is incapable of understanding what he feels. Tom replies that he would be sorry to understand, but only wishes to be understood that he will thrash Philip if he comes near Maggie again. Philip says that if Maggie wishes to give him up, he will abide by that. Maggie says that she must for her father's sake. Tom snatches Maggie away.

When they have parted, Maggie tells Tom she detests his "insulting unmanly allusions" to Philip's deformity; she says his mind is not large enough to see anything better than his own conduct. She refuses to defend herself but says that if Tom were ever at fault, she would be sorry for him, whereas he has no pity. She says she would not give up Philip in obedience to him but only for her father.

Tom returns to St. Ogg's, and Maggie goes to her room and cries. She sees now that she is not "above worldly temptations," and she is pained for the insults Philip had to bear. Yet, she feels "a certain dim background of relief" which she thinks is due to "deliverance from concealment."

Commentary

Philip appears in his best light in this chapter. By assigning to Tom a feeling of repugnance at Philip's deformity, the author tends to kill that feeling in the reader. The interview between the two reflects better on Philip than on Tom. He obviously cares more about Maggie than Tom does. Nonetheless, Tom's accusations are not without effect: "You know well enough what sort of justice and cherishing you were preparing for her." This has effect because of the ambivalence with which Philip has been treated all along.

Tom's early severity with Maggie is becoming more and more strong. He is not willing to sacrifice "justice" with her even for his father's peace of mind. He forces her to "renounce all private speech and intercourse with Philip Wakem from this time forth. Else you will bring shame on us all, and grief on my father." Yet he himself is willing to inform his father if Maggie will not do as he wishes.

By contrast, Maggie thinks only of her father now. "Tom threatens to tell my father—and he couldn't bear it," she tells Philip. She cares for people, while Tom cares for abstract principles. One of Tom's statements expresses this central characteristic of his: "I should be very sorry to understand your feelings," he tells Philip.

The final paragraph of the chapter reinforces the uneasiness about the relationship of Maggie and Philip. It is ambivalent because it is in Maggie's point of view, and it carries the implication that she really cared for Philip only because she *should*.

CHAPTER 6

Summary

It is three weeks later when Tom comes home early, in a good humor, and asks his father to count their money. Mr. Tulliver is sure of the amount, but he does as his son wishes. The amount comes out as he expected, with three hundred pounds still needed for his debts. Mr. Tulliver fears he will not live that long. Tom tells his father that the debts can be paid with his own hand, for he has saved over three hundred pounds from his own trade. Tulliver is struck silent and finally breaks into tears. He is triumphant that Wakem will know of it, for Tom has arranged a dinner to pay the creditors, and it has been advertised in the paper. They drink to this success, and Tulliver insists on hearing all the details over and over. He cannot sleep well that night, and early in the morning he wakens, dreaming that he has Wakem in his grasp.

Commentary

Mr. Tulliver is no longer the man of the family. That position has been taken by Tom. When Mr. Tulliver speaks to him it is with "rather timid discontent." But Tulliver's single-mindedness in revenge is still the thing which most affects his son. Tulliver's dream of revenge prepares for the actual attack he is to make on Wakem.

Mrs. Tulliver's "much-reduced bunch of keys" is symbolic of her lower state in the world but also of the characteristics which she still retains, the Dodson caution and concern with material things.

CHAPTER 7

Summary

At dinner with his creditors, Tulliver looks like his old self. He makes a long speech about his honesty and his admiration for his son. Tom makes a brief speech, giving thanks for the honor done him, and is well received. Tulliver rides home on the main street, "with uplifted head and free glances," wishing he would meet Wakem. They do meet, at the gate to the mill yard. Wakem makes a harsh comment on Tulliver's farming. Tulliver says angrily that he will "serve no longer under a scoundrel," and when Wakem tries to pass, Tulliver knocks him from his horse. He is whipping Wakem when Maggie comes to restrain him.

Luke helps Wakem to his horse, while Maggie helps her father to his bed, for he is faint and pale. A half-hour later Tom comes home. He is dejected that his "exemplary effort" is confounded by this occurrence.

No one is worried about Mr. Tulliver, but in the early morning Tom and Maggie are wakened by their mother: the doctor has been sent for, and their father has asked for them. When they come in, Mr. Tulliver asks Tom to try to get the mill back and charges him to care for his mother and be good to Maggie, as he had been good to *his* sister. At last he says, with difficulty, that he has had his turn and beat Wakem. Maggie begs him to forgive Wakem, but Tulliver says he cannot "love a raskill." He subsides into mutterings, and the doctor arrives an hour later only to pronounce him dead. Tom and Maggie cling together and promise to love each other.

Commentary

Note that Tom feels as much self-pity at having the edge taken off his success as sorrow for his father. "Tom was dejected by the thought that

his exemplary effort must always be baffled by the wrong-doing of others
...." Maggie, once again, feels only sympathy for her father.

On his deathbed Tulliver charges Tom to be good to Maggie. This is
the one charge he later forgets, or misunderstands, although he remembers fully the mission of revenge. Yet, while Tom does not have his father's
generosity, he is like his father in one matter of principle: his ground for
turning out Maggie is ironically of the same type as Tulliver's refusal to
forgive Wakem—"I can't love a raskill...."

BOOK SIX: THE GREAT TEMPTATION

CHAPTER 1

Summary

Lucy Deane is being courted by Stephen Guest, son of the principal
partner of Guest and Company. He is a handsome, apparently flippant
young man. Lucy is telling him that she has important news. He guesses
that it is about her dog's diet or Dr. Kenn "preaching against buckram";
but she informs him that her cousin Maggie is coming to stay with her. At
the same time she worries aloud that Maggie will object to seeing Philip
Wakem, who often comes to sing glees with Stephen and Lucy. Stephen is
annoyed that Lucy is to have company, but he inquires about the ground
of Maggie's dislike for Philip. Lucy tells him what little she knows of the
old quarrel between Tulliver and Wakem. She says that Maggie has been
"in a dreary situation in a school" since Mr. Tulliver's death. This is to be
her first holiday. It will allow Maggie to be near her mother, who has been
housekeeper for Lucy and Mr. Deane since the death of Mrs. Deane.
Stephen expects that Maggie will be like her mother—"a fat blonde girl,
with round blue eyes, who will stare at us silently." Lucy says that that is
Maggie exactly.

Stephen goes to the piano and asks Lucy to sing with him. After several songs Stephen departs, leaving Lucy with "an inclination to walk up
and down the room." She sees to the preparation of Maggie's room, and
half forgets "her own happy love-affairs."

Stephen Guest is of the opinion that this is the sort of woman to
marry—a woman thoughtful of other women, pretty but "not to a madden-
ing extent," gentle and "not stupid." He must overcome a slight unwilling-
ness in his father and sisters, but he means to do so.

Commentary

Note how Stephen is immediately connected with music images. He is constantly singing, humming, standing at the piano. Philip has been Maggie's main connection with music in the past, but now his status is weakened as Stephen's strengthens. Philip becomes "our only apology for a tenor." Stephen, by contrast, sings "with admirable ease." Music is made a symbol for courtship: "Surely the only courtship unshaken by doubts and fears, must be that in which the lovers can sing together." Lovers "believed what they sang all the more *because* they sang it," and we are told of the "loving chase of a fugue."

Like Philip, Stephen is treated with a certain ambivalence. He never really recovers from the frivolous air he has when we first see him: "Mr. Stephen Guest, whose diamond ring, attar of roses, and air of nonchalant leisure, at twelve o'clock in the day, are the graceful and odoriferous results of the largest oil-mill and the most extensive wharf in St. Ogg's. There is an apparent triviality in the action with the scissors...." This triviality is never entirely forgotten. It is picked up again in a contrast with Tom's business-like manner when Stephen relates that Tom saved the company from a considerable loss but that he cannot recall the details because he "was rather drowsy at the time."

Lucy is a believable character in spite of being of a type we might expect to be dull – the good, innocent friend. Her innocence is emphasized: her affair with Stephen is "a duet in Paradise." She is tiny, loving, "fond of feeding dependent creatures." She is made believable partly through being seen at first through Stephen's eyes, who makes her acceptable as "a woman who was loving and thoughtful for other women, not giving them Judas-kisses with eyes askance on their welcome defects...."

Note that the time is now two years after Mr. Tulliver's death. Maggie has been "in a situation" as governess.

CHAPTER 2

Summary

Lucy tells Maggie how clever Stephen is and hopes she will like him. She says he is too good for her, and Maggie replies playfully that if she disapproves of him then Lucy can give him up. Lucy hopes Maggie will not be disappointed. She expects Stephen to be surprised, and she remarks on how beautiful Maggie is, even in shabby clothes.

Maggie has been poor and hard-worked, and Lucy promises to get her into the habit of being happy. The old scenes are pleasant to Maggie, and Lucy has prepared "a riotous feast" of music. She tactfully brings up the fact that Philip Wakem is to sing with them. Maggie assures her that she does not dislike Philip as Tom does; but before she can explain further, she is interrupted by Stephen's entry.

Stephen is quite astonished by this dark-haired, intelligent woman. He covers his confusion in a florid compliment. Maggie sees that he has been satirical about her, and she answers somewhat defiantly that he has said what was necessary to say. This "alarming amount of devil" attracts Stephen. Lucy is afraid that they are going to dislike each other, for they continue to speak rather sharply. To forestall embarrassment, Stephen begins to speak to Lucy about the bazaar which is to be held the next month. The talk changes to Dr. Kenn, the clergyman who "gives away two-thirds of his income" and who Stephen thinks is "one of the finest fellows in the world"; and then to Stephen's hopes of standing for election to parliament; and then on to books. Stephen waxes clever, hoping to impress Maggie. At last he suggests that they go rowing. While Maggie goes for her bonnet, Lucy tells Stephen to bring Philip the next day. She asks whether Stephen doesn't find Maggie "a dear, noble-looking creature." Stephen replies that she is not his type. Lucy believes him, but is determined that Maggie will not know it.

Stephen calculates the chances of getting Maggie to take his hand in entering the boat. He believes that he finds Maggie interesting, but that he could never love her. However, he is disappointed when Maggie fails to look at him in the boat. When they step out of the boat, Maggie slips and Stephen steadies her. Maggie has never before felt what it is "to be taken care of...by someone taller and stronger than one's self."

When they reach home, Mr. and Mrs. Pullet are there. Stephen hurries away. Aunt Pullett is shocked at Maggie's shabby clothes and promises to give her some of her own. There is a general discussion of the shape of Maggie's arms and their darkness. Lucy defends her color, saying a painter would find her complexion beautiful. Maggie thinks that so much talk on that subject will drive her crazy, like uncle Pullet's song about the "Nut-brown Maid."

Commentary

" 'Oh, then, if I disapprove of him, you can give him up, since you are not engaged,' said Maggie, with playful gravity." This is ironic in view of later events; but it also contains the key to what Maggie might have done but fails to think of. Somehow she never considers later that she might ask Stephen to settle matters with Lucy.

The author makes it clear that Stephen is instantly impressed with Maggie, perhaps even more than he realizes himself. Although he cannot keep his eyes off her, he dismisses her to himself with the thought that "one is not obliged to marry such women." His thought that he had certainly not fallen in love with her is far more certain than his actions indicate.

Maggie for her part finds it "very charming" to be taken care of by a strong man. The contrast with Philip, both in physical impression and in Maggie's reaction, is obvious.

Dr. Kenn is introduced through a conversation about him. In this way his goodness is left in no doubt. He is "a man who has eight hundred a-year, and is contented with deal furniture and boiled beef because he gives away two-thirds of his income." The introduction of Dr. Kenn here is purely plot preparation. It makes him a familiar character later when he is needed as a refuge for Maggie.

CHAPTER 3

Summary

Maggie is unable to sleep that night because of the memory of Stephen's singing and his glances. The feelings aroused by the music, the "presence of a world of love and beauty and delight," remain with her. At length Lucy comes to talk to her. She asks what Maggie thinks of Stephen, and is told that he is too self-confident. Lucy says that Philip is to come the next day. Maggie tells Lucy she cannot see Philip without Tom's leave. She finds it necessary to tell Lucy that she has promised not to see Philip again, and finally Lucy pries from her the story of her connection with Philip. Lucy finds it "very beautiful," and she sets out to find a way to bring them together again. At this Maggie shivers, "as if she felt a sudden chill."

Commentary

Music to Maggie is made of "wild passion and fancy," and it is emphasized that she has been strongly affected by "hearing some fine music sung by a fine bass voice"—a voice we know to be Stephen's. "Life seems to go on without effort, when I am filled with music." Note that later it is an effortless mode of existence, for which she longs, which lulls Maggie into acquiescence with Stephen's plan to elope. Their love affair is largely expressed in images such as these. Music and effortless delight, things which Maggie renounced in her early religious faith, are the things she most closely associates with Stephen and her love for him.

When Maggie confesses to Lucy that she loves Philip, the author hints twice that this is less than true. At the suggestion that she may be able to marry Philip, "Maggie tried to smile, but shivered, as if she felt a sudden chill." This represents the thought, still unconscious in her, that she really cannot love Philip. The second hint of trouble to come is the author's statement that, although Maggie had been sincere, "confidences are sometimes blinding, even when they are sincere." Maggie means what she says, but Lucy continues to believe that Maggie loves Philip even after it ceases to be true.

Lucy is still thought of as a child, a "pretty spaniel"; but her character is being more and more fully developed. Her reaction to Maggie's plight is predictable, but it is mature. Only her faith and loyalty are childlike.

CHAPTER 4

Summary

Tom is lodging with Bob Jakin. When Maggie goes to visit him, she is met by Bob's wife. The woman is excited to meet Maggie. She rushes off to the back of the house to find Bob, who tells Maggie that Tom is "glumpish" and sits at home staring at the fire except when he is at work. Bob believes that Tom has "a soft place in him," for he has made a great effort to find a black spaniel. This is the dog which was presented to Lucy. Maggie is doubtful that this signifies that Tom is in love.

When Tom comes in, he speaks coldly. Maggie asks to be absolved of her promise not to see Philip, and Tom agrees, still more coldly. Maggie tells him it is for Lucy's sake, but Tom says that she will have to give up her brother if she begins to think of Philip as a lover. He says he has no confidence in her. Maggie finds this cruel and cannot keep back her tears. Tom speaks more kindly then, telling her that she lacks judgment and will not be guided. He says he did not wish her "to take a situation," but would have supported her as a lady and that he can never feel certain of what she will do. Maggie says in return that she has given up Philip, and will be only his friend. It is unreasonable of Tom to condemn her for faults not yet committed, Tom admits at last that it would be best for her not to object to seeing Philip.

Commentary

Maggie considers Bob's hint that Tom is in love with Lucy "perhaps a mere fancy of Bob's too officious brain"; and in fact the reference leads nowhere. The only further development is Lucy's certainty that she can get Tom to agree to a marriage between Maggie and Philip. This reference may be the vestige of a plot development which the author decided not to use.

Tom's attitude to Maggie is still one of stern righteousness, rather than generous love. He says, "I wished my sister to be a lady, and I would always have taken care of you, as my father desired, until you were well married." He remembers his father's injunction, but he cannot comprehend its spirit. He lacks the generosity his father showed toward Mrs. Moss. He sees "caring for" Maggie in terms of money and obedience, not love. (This may be contrasted to Bob Jakin's generosity to Maggie after Tom turns her out.)

Nevertheless, Tom sees a side of Maggie's character which is easy to overlook. The author calls it "that hard rind of truth which is discerned by unimaginative, unsympathetic minds." Because Tom is so unsympathetic, we are disinclined to accept his judgment that Maggie "would be led away to do anything"; but later he is seen to be right.

CHAPTER 5

Summary

Uncle Deane calls Tom in to talk about a trip Tom is to make for the firm. He goes on to speak of the increasingly good trade opportunities, the seven years Tom has served the firm, and his general satisfaction with his nephew. Finally he tells Tom that he and Mr. Guest have decided to offer Tom a share in the business. Tom is properly grateful, but he takes the opportunity to state his belief that Dorlcote Mill would be a good investment for the company. He requests that, if it can be bought, he be given the management of the mill and the chance to buy it by working off the price. Tom says that Wakem may part with it, since the present manager, Jetsome, has taken to drinking. Mr. Deane promises to see what can be done.

Commentary

The chapter is mainly preparation for events to come — Tom's recovery of the mill and the bargain between Philip and his father to help Philip marry Maggie by returning the mill to Tom. However, Mr. Deane's discourse throws light on Tom's character and on Stephen's. Tom, like Mr. Deane, is efficiently practical, but his interests have narrowed to the exclusion of all but business. Stephen is clever, "considering he's seen nothing of business." He is clever in an idle refined way.

CHAPTER 6

Summary

When Maggie is launched by Lucy into St. Ogg's society, she becomes the subject of much interest from the men and from the women who comment on her unpretentiousness (but without the vulgarity of the rest of "poor Lucy's relations"). Maggie is enchanted by "this new sense of leisure" and the feeling that she is "one of the beautiful things of this spring-time." She begins to study at the piano again and ceases to think of the future.

Philip had not come when expected. He was gone from home and returns only after twelve days. In the meantime Maggie has become "oppressively conscious" of Stephen's presence, and he of hers. On the day of Philip's return, Lucy promises to spend the evening with Mrs. Kenn, who is in ill health and needs help with the bazaar which is to take place shortly. It is understood that Stephen will not come that evening, but as Maggie is sitting in the drawing room after dinner, Stephen comes in from the garden. He tells her he has brought some music for Lucy. He sits by Maggie. Neither one is able to speak. At last he mentions that Philip is due back. The name disperses the spell Maggie feels under, and she takes up some sewing. She drops some yarn, and when Stephen retrieves it the glance they exchange unsettles him. He starts to go, then asks her to walk a little way in the garden. He offers his arm, and the firm support is "strangely winning" to Maggie. A word from Stephen rouses her, and she retreats to the house, wishing she and Philip were together again in the Red Deeps.

Stephen spends the evening in a billiards room thinking of Maggie and reminding himself that this is madness.

Commentary

The Gleggs and Pullets have heretofore been seen only through Dodson eyes. They are now seen through the eyes of higher society, and they appear considerably smaller. To the Miss Guests, "it was not agreeable to think of any connection by marriage with such peoples as the Gleggs and the Pullets."

There is a central statement of the meaning of the music images which have been used in connection with Maggie: "her sensibility to the supreme excitement of music was only one form of that passionate sensibility which belonged to her whole nature, and made her faults and virtues all merge in each other...." Note too the specific use of the river image here: "Maggie's destiny...like the course of an unmapped river: we only know that the river is full and rapid, and that for all rivers there is the same final home."

Stephen and Maggie are still unaware of the true nature of their attraction for one another. Their love, like the music which expresses it, is a spontaneous thing which goes against the wishes of both.

Once again Stephen is contrasted to Philip by "that offer of the firm arm: the help is not wanted physically at that moment, but the sense of help—the presence of strength that is outside them and yet theirs, meets a continual want of the imagination."

Lucy is drawn in two dimensions in order that she will not occupy the reader's awareness at Maggie's expense. The difference between the reader's awareness and Lucy's is made a source of irony: "Lucy was very happy: all the happier because Stephen's society seemed to have become much more interesting and amusing since Maggie had been there." The author uses this to reflect on Lucy's "tranquil-hearted" nature. This is important because in the end Lucy's innocence is the one thing which makes Maggie's renunciation of Stephen seem right. Her treatment of Philip is hardly a betrayal, even in his own eyes, but Lucy is so pure and harmless that she requires special consideration.

CHAPTER 7

Summary

The next morning is rainy, and Lucy expects Stephen to come earlier. But instead it is Philip who comes. He and Maggie meet with inward agitation. After some "artificial conversation" Maggie tells him that Tom has consented to their being friends, but that she will soon go away "to a new situation." After he begs her to stay and she insists on going, Philip tells her she is returning to renunciation to find "an escape from pain." The love in Philip's face makes Maggie conscience-stricken; she wonders whether he is remembering what she does, the thing he once said about "a lover of Lucy's." But when Philip asks if something is wrong, she says not.

Stephen arrives just then, Philip is oppressed by his "bright strong presence and strong voice." Stephen and Maggie are barely polite to each other, and each is hurt by the other's coldness. To brighten the situation Lucy suggests music. Philip plays the piano as he and Stephen sing. Maggie cannot help feeling moved by the music. Lucy requests more, and Philip, "not quite unintentionally," begins to play "I love thee still," a song he has sung to Maggie before. It makes Maggie feel "regret in the place of excitement." But when Stephen begins to sing, Maggie is "borne along by a wave too strong for her." After some minutes Maggie walks across the room for a footstool. Stephen fetches it for her, and the glance they exchange is "delicious to both." Philip sees it and he feels "a vague anxiety."

Mr. Deane comes in, and the music breaks off. He asks Philip about his father's farming. Lucy is curious at this, and that night at dinner she asks him about it. Her father tells her that the firm may wish to buy the mill. He asks her to say nothing about it. Lucy says that if he will allow her to speak to Philip, she believes she can make certain that Mr. Wakem will sell the mill. Since Mr. Deane sees little chance otherwise, he agrees.

Commentary

Several things help ease the reader's acceptance of Maggie's new love. When Philip re-enters, even Lucy "could not resist the impression that her cousin Tom had some excuse for feeling shocked at the physical incongruity between the two...." Even Philip's good points are weakened: his "resolute suppression of emotion" is indicated by a "high, feeble voice." The physical comparison is favorable to Stephen, and the imagery is too. During the singing, "when her soul was being played on," it is chiefly Stephen's voice which affects Maggie. Philip's "pleading tenor had no very fine qualities as a voice." When Stephen sings directly to her, she is "borne along by a wave too strong for her." (When, in Chapter 13, she goes with Stephen to marry him, she will be both literally and metaphorically "borne along by the tide.")

In the midst of this first meeting, Maggie remembers what Philip had once said "about a lover of Lucy's." This is a reminder of the earlier meeting (Book V, Chapter 4) where he jested that she would "avenge the dark women in your own person, and carry away all the love from your cousin Lucy." Philip immediately recognizes that Maggie and Stephen are in love, but he will not allow himself to believe it yet. Nevertheless, he is oppressed by Stephen's presence and strength. But if Philip's weakness is emphasized, so is his honor. He will not believe the worst, and he refuses to speak of love because "it would have seemed to him like reminding Maggie of a promise." As his suitability as a match for Maggie is degraded, his clear understanding and knowledge of human nature are emphasized. In the end, it is he who enables us to see Maggie — and himself — most clearly.

CHAPTER 8

Summary

Lucy speaks privately with Philip, who lays a plan to remove his father as an obstacle between himself and Maggie. He asks his father to come up to his studio to see some new sketches. Among them are several studies of Maggie. When Mr. Wakem discovers who they are, he questions Philip about his relationship with Maggie. Philip tells him their past history, and says that he would marry her if she would have him. Mr. Wakem is enraged at this return for his "indulgences"; but Philip says he did not think a return was required. Mr. Wakem says Philip can marry her if he pleases and go his way. But he waits for a reply, which is that Philip is unable to support himself and will not offer her poverty. He says his father has the power to deprive him of his one chance of happiness, if he wishes. However, Maggie has never entered her family's quarrels, and resentment is ridiculous. Wakem says that what women do is of less concern than whom they belong to. At this Philip becomes angry for the first time. He defends Maggie as being more than his equal and says she might not have him anyway. Wakem storms out, and Philip goes out to avoid meeting him again at once. He returns in the evening. He is dozing in his studio when his father enters. Mr. Wakem asks Philip if Maggie loves him. Philip replies that she once said so but that she was very young, and he does not wish to force her. Mr. Wakem has seen Maggie and thinks her handsome. He reminisces about his own wife, whom he apparently loved very much.

With that barrier down, Philip is able to get his father's agreement to sell the mill. When Lucy reports this to her father, Mr. Deane is puzzled, but he does not care to pry too closely into the matter.

Commentary

Here, as later, Philip provides the means to understand the author's meaning. A comment of his may be used as a measure of all the human relationships in the book. He tells his father he does not regard his own life as a return for his father's care. "You have been an indulgent father to me; but I have always felt that it was because you had an affectionate wish to give me as much happiness as my unfortunate lot would admit of—not that it was a debt you expected me to pay by sacrificing all my chance of happiness to satisfy feelings of yours, which I can never share." This is especially pertinent to the relationship of Tom and Maggie in comparison to that between Maggie and her father.

Mr. Wakem states one of the axioms of his society, one which is most applicable to Maggie's case: "We don't ask what a woman does—we ask whom she belongs to." Maggie's cleverness has always been a handicap to her. Later, "what she does" in another sense is made less important to the world than whom she belongs to: running away with Stephen would have been acceptable if she had married him; because she does not, she is made an outcast.

Mr. Wakem takes on new stature through his love for his dead wife. He has previously been a character of interest but of little depth. Here he becomes a human being.

CHAPTER 9

Summary

On the day of the bazaar Maggie helps Lucy in a booth selling "certain large plain articles." These include gentlemen's dressing gowns, which become the center of much attention. The notice thus drawn to Maggie insures that it will later be recalled that there was something "rather bold" about her. Stephen purchases nothing from Maggie until Lucy asks him to. Mr. Wakem speaks to Maggie quite amiably, and he is just leaving as Stephen comes up. Both Maggie and Stephen feel triumphant that they have been able to disregard one another, but Maggie's imminent departure makes "self-conquest in detail" unnecessary. Still, they feel unable to avoid one another now. As they are speaking, Stephen notices Philip watching them. He goes to speak to him, but Philip angrily calls him a hypocrite. Stephen goes off to another room to be alone with his emotions, while Maggie sits struggling with herself.

Maggie is approached by Dr. Kenn, who observes that there is something wrong. He offers his services if he can help. Maggie says nothing, but she is feeling that her choice would be to "have Stephen Guest at her feet." She longs for that life of ease, but she cannot accept it for herself. Philip has said nothing to her, although Lucy has told her that Tom will regain the mill. Now Lucy tries to dissuade her from going to visit her aunt Moss. Instead, Maggie says that she must go, for she is soon going to take a new position as a teacher. Lucy protests that there is now nothing to keep her and Philip apart, but Maggie reminds her that there is Tom's feeling. Lucy promises to speak to Tom, and asks if Maggie truly loves Philip. Maggie says that she would choose to marry him, if it were not for Tom.

Commentary

Local society is treated in some depth in order to give a background against which the main characters may be seen. Society's view of Maggie is emphasized, and future events are foreshadowed by the hint of a later change in that view: "...it is possible that the emphatic notice of various kinds which was drawn towards Miss Tulliver on this public occasion, threw a very strong and unmistakeable light on her subsequent conduct in many minds then present."

The author spells out her conception of how Stephen is to be regarded: "Stephen was not a hypocrite—capable of deliberate doubleness for a selfish end...." The explanation is offered as an antidote to Philip's jealous beliefs.

Dr. Kenn, on this first appearance, makes no definite impression. He is obviously perceptive; his "ear and eye took in all the signs that this brief confidence of Maggie's was charged with meaning." But he draws no conclusions from it other than that "she has some trouble or other at heart." Now, as later, Dr. Kenn is strictly a foil for Maggie's emotions and position.

The fruits of Maggie's early life may be seen in her reactions now. She longs for a life of luxury and culture, "but there were things in her stronger than vanity—passion, and affection, and long deep memories of early discipline and effort, of early claims on her love and pity...." Her character now is clearly a product of what we have seen of her childhood, and we are not surprised at her wish to get away from Stephen. Yet, as always, she cannot suppress her emotions entirely, and so she is forced to use Tom's prejudice against Philip as an excuse to delay Lucy's plans.

CHAPTER 10

Summary

There is a dance at Park House, Stephen's home. Maggie at first refuses to dance, but at length the music persuades her, even though her partner is "the horrible young Torry." Stephen has not asked her to dance, for he feels Philip's attachment to her to be "another claim of honour"; but the sight of her with Torry is too much for him to resist. He makes his way to her and asks her to walk out with him. Maggie says little but in the conservatory she reaches for a rose, and Stephen impulsively kisses her arm. She indignantly darts from him. Stephen follows to ask her forgiveness, but Maggie sends him away.

Maggie feels that this moment has set her free from the possibility of treachery to Lucy.

The next morning Maggie is to go to visit aunt Moss. Philip comes before she leaves. He reminds her of their earlier days. When she tells him she is going away, he asks if they can ever come together again. She replies that only Tom separates them now. Philip persists, asking if that is the only reason. She says it is, and believes it. But despite Philip's faith in Maggie, he is unable to be completely happy with her answer.

Commentary

"The horrible young Torry" is here only a personification of masculine reaction to Maggie in St. Ogg's society. He is not a person, but a stage property useful in furthering the action. Later he will be made symbolic of St. Ogg's reaction to Maggie's elopement.

Maggie's emotional reactions are still immature. She goes to extremes easily. Stephen's kiss is to her "a horrible punishment...come upon her for the sin of allowing a moment's happiness that was treachery to Lucy, to Philip—to her own better soul." This reaction is exactly like that by which she later renounces Stephen once and for all. It is a moral reaction, but one founded on her own conception of morality. She will not do anything that will bring pain to others, and her idea of pain to others is an extreme one. But, as always, Maggie overrates her own powers of renunciation. She believes that "this scorching moment...had delivered her from the possibility of another word or look that would have the stamp of treachery towards that gentle, unsuspicious sister." The author hints plainly that it had not.

CHAPTER 11

Summary

Maggie has spent four days with her aunt before Stephen comes to see her. She is walking with Mrs. Moss when Stephen rides up. He asks to speak to Maggie privately. They walk together into the lane, where Maggie says his coming is not gentlemanly and she will go no farther. Stephen says it is not right that she should treat one who is mad with love for her as if he were "a coarse brute, who would willingly offend" her. Maggie asks him not to say those things. Stephen asks her forgiveness for the other evening. She grants it and asks him again to leave. He says he cannot, unless she will go a little way with him. She walks on with him, trying to tell him that this is wicked because of Lucy and Philip. Stephen says if Maggie loves him, they should be married. Maggie would "rather die than fall into that temptation," but she cannot deny that she loves Stephen. He asks her again to marry him. He says they are breaking no "positive engagement." When Maggie says that in that case "there would be no such thing as faithfulness," he argues that to pretend to care for Philip and Lucy is wrong to them as well. Maggie says that some duties come before love. She convinces Stephen that they must part, and they exchange one kiss.

Commentary

The author has pictured Stephen as a dapper young man, strong and handsome and clever, but with little self-knowledge. In humbling himself to

Maggie, Stephen is meant to achieve a new depth of character—but this is not entirely successful. The centering of interest on Maggie allows too little time and concentration on Stephen for him to bear the burden placed on him. He fails to measure up fully as Maggie's lover, and most readers will not share Maggie's infatuation with him.

Maggie sees the central problem of her own position, and the question with which the book is now concerned is the truth of that position—"that I must not, cannot seek my own happiness by sacrificing others." Maggie will go to great extremes to avoid injuring others. At times she seems trapped within a code as strict as that of the Dodsons, although it is of her own making and based on personal relationships, not on tradition.

Note the image of this love against which Maggie struggles—a "current, soft and yet strong as the summer stream." This comes to fulfillment in the real current which carries her away with Stephen.

CHAPTER 12

Summary

At the end of the week Maggie goes to visit aunt Pullet. A party is being held there to celebrate Tom's acquisition of the mill. Lucy comes early in order to talk to Maggie and to convince aunt Pullet that she should donate some things to Tom and his mother to make their housekeeping easier. Mrs. Pullet finally agrees to give up some of her linen, but she says she will not save any for Maggie as the girl insists on "going into service." Maggie's employment is a sore point with her family, who all wish her to come live with them now that she is "capable of being at once ornamental and useful." Mrs. Glegg is indignant that Maggie does not do her duty to her aunts but "settles to go away" without their knowledge. However, she is unwilling to have Maggie come stay with her, as that would involve opening another room. Instead, she insists that Maggie visit her every morning.

Tom is welcomed warmly, and reminded that he owes his success to the good example of his mother's family.

Lucy contrives to have Tom drive her home with his mother after the party. She counts on this chance to get his consent for Maggie to marry Philip. But all she accomplishes is to make Tom think that Maggie is going to change one "perverse resolve...into something equally perverse, but entirely different...." Tom refuses his blessing, although he says Maggie may do as she likes.

Commentary

The excellence of characterization of the Dodson sisters is partly due to the code which underlies their individual natures, for while each has her own peculiarities, they are recognizably in character at all times through their family similarities. Mrs. Glegg is the one in whom the code is most strict, but she is also the most sensible. She tells her sister that "locking in and out" is going too far: "You go beyond your own family. There's nobody can say I don't lock up; but I do what's reasonable, and no more." This is largely true. She is strict, but she has fewer silly mannerisms than the rest of the family.

Note the recurrence of references to the importance of a proper death and of the "key" images.

Lucy's suggestion to Tom that Maggie be allowed to marry Philip is of course refused, "notwithstanding Lucy's power over her strong-willed cousin." This is the last reference to Tom's special love for her. The earlier hints lead only to this. It may be taken as a special illustration of his character that his idea of right is stronger even than this love. It is perfectly in accord with the author's analysis of Tom here: "strength of will, conscious rectitude of purpose, narrowness of imagination and intellect, great power of self-control, and a disposition to exert control over others." In all ways he is the opposite of Maggie.

CHAPTER 13

Summary

Maggie escapes Stephen by remaining at aunt Glegg's each day after her return to St. Ogg's, but she is forced to see him each evening. He has taken to dining with the Deanes, despite his resolution to keep away. Maggie is tempted by her desire for Stephen, but she will not let herself inflict pain on Lucy and Philip. But because they are soon to part, both Maggie and Stephen feel that small signs of mutual love are harmless. Philip comes infrequently, but he is there one evening when Lucy suggests that Maggie would like to go boating more often. She persuades Philip to come rowing with them the next day. Stephen moodily declines to come, for he does not wish to share Maggie's company. Philip senses this and offers not to come, but Stephen says he will row the day after.

Philip does not like to doubt Maggie, but when he sees Maggie blush at a word from Stephen, he finds it impossible to resist his suspicion. He comes to the belief that Maggie is planning to go away in order to escape from her love for Stephen. A night of worry leaves him too ill for boating the next day. He sends a note to Stephen asking that Stephen take his place.

Lucy meanwhile has arranged "a charming plan" to throw Philip and Maggie together. She decides to go to a neighboring town to make "important purchases." Maggie is content to be alone with Philip. She is startled when Stephen comes instead. She first refuses to go with him, but he persuades her at last. The river carries them swiftly downstream with little effort. They speak little until Maggie sees that they have passed Luckreth, their destination. She is frightened then, for they will be unable to get home for hours. Stephen then asks Maggie to continue with him and be married. He says that "everything has concurred" to help them. Maggie refuses, saying that Stephen has taken advantage of her thoughtlessness. He denies that he intended it, but says that he can send her home from here, so that the blame will be all his. Maggie feels that she has been too harsh, and he feels "all the relenting in her look and tone." He moves to her side and lets the boat drift, while Maggie is content in "having everything decided for her."

Stephen sees a vessel coming downriver, and he proposes that they board it and land at Mudport "or any convenient place on the coast." Maggie does not refuse, for "one course seemed as difficult as another." Stephen hails the boat and tells them he and his wife have come out too far and are fatigued. They are taken up. Then it is too late for Maggie to do anything but wait for tomorrow. Stephen is triumphant, for he now believes that they will never be parted. But Maggie falls asleep with the sense that "the morrow must bring back the old life of struggle."

Commentary

Maggie is borne along by the tide both literally and metaphorically. Note the continual references to the drift being due to a power beyond Maggie and Stephen's control. To Maggie, Stephen is "this stronger presence that seemed to bear her along without any act of her own will." They "glided rapidly along...helped by the backward-flowing tide." The boat "glided without his help." Maggie's emotional drift is of the same nature. She is "yearning...that she might glide along with the swift, silent stream, and not struggle any more." Comparing her emotional drift to an unstoppable action makes the love affair, and her capitulation, seem more reasonable. At the same time, she knows that an act of will can overcome this: she is reminding herself that this is "cruel selfishness." Her first thoughts are of others – she is in agony over what Lucy will think. When she does yield, it is to alleviate Stephen's suffering "because it was less distinguishable from that sense of others' claims which was the moral basis of her resistance." She is yearning for a life "in which affection would no longer be self-sacrifice." This is an attempt to turn a dream to reality, like her attempt to run away to the gypsies. She wants to "annul the wretched facts."

Still another characteristic of Maggie's early life is used to make this situation more believable. "At all times she was so liable to fits of absence, that she was likely enough to let her way-marks pass unnoticed." This has been demonstrated several times.

A remark of Philip's foreshadows this occurrence: he says that if Maggie loves rowing too much she will be "selling her soul to that ghostly boatman who haunts the Floss—only for the sake of being drifted in a boat forever." This is what she wants—to give up "the old life of struggle," and be "lulled to sleep with that soft stream still flowing over her...."

Philip's jealousy is used to control the direction of the reader's thoughts and fears. He recognizes that Maggie is "banishing herself," and he raises the possibility that Stephen will not give her up, knowing "that she was made half helpless by her feeling towards him." Philip's own actions here are based on the self-sacrifice which Maggie holds to be the basis of moral conduct; but he acts in a more sensible way than she does. "He would not trust himself to see her, till he had assured himself that he could act from pure anxiety for her, and not from egoistic irritation."

CHAPTER 14

Summary

Maggie awakes from a dream that she has been on the water with Stephen and has seen the boat of St. Ogg with the Virgin seated in it. The Virgin becomes Lucy and the boatman Philip and then Tom, who rows past without looking. She calls to him, and they begin to sink. She dreams she wakes as a child, then wakes to reality. She feels that she has committed an "irrevocable wrong," and that life with Stephen "could have no sacredness." She sees Stephen asleep on the deck close to her, and she feels that the worst bitterness is the pain she must give to him. To delay that as long as possible, she says nothing of parting until they come to Mudport.

When Maggie says she must return, Stephen vows to die first. They go into an inn and Stephen orders a carriage, but Maggie insists that they must part. Stephen tries to tell her that it is too late, that whatever damage will be done is done already, and that "constancy without love" is useless. But Maggie argues that the past must bind them, and that she could not live at peace with herself if she were to commit a willful sin. Stephen cries that her love is nothing, for he could commit crimes for her, while she is robbing him of his "life's happiness." She rejects his argument that their position has changed since the previous day, for the fact that she has made others suffer would embitter their love. Stephen says she does not know what will be said when she returns, but Maggie replies that Lucy and Philip will believe her. Stephen lets her go at last, angry for the moment.

Maggie gets into a coach, but it takes her farther from home. She spends the night at York, half-sick with anguish, intending to start home the next day.

Commentary

Maggie's dream represents her dearest wish—that Tom will not be really angry. It foreshadows their ultimate reconciliation at the time of their drowning.

The problem Maggie confronts herself with is a conflict of duty and desire. "She had rent the ties that had given meaning to duty, and had made herself an outlawed soul, with no guide but the wayward choice of her own passion." The problem is a real one, and there are good arguments on either side. Stephen is right to ask, "Would they have thanked us for anything so hollow as constancy without love?" We have already seen that Philip would not. Maggie is no doubt right to answer that "faithfulness and constancy mean...renouncing whatever is opposed to the reliance others have in us—whatever would cause misery to those whom the course of our lives has made dependent on us." But it seems clear that she greatly overestimates her own power to avoid hurting others. Hers is a sentimental yearning for the right. She acts without considering what she can really do; she acts impulsively, as always. Yet, Maggie is right that she could never be happy if she gave up her best impulses. Maggie does not fully realize, as Stephen does, how much their position is altered. In trying to regain what she had before, Maggie is fighting an impossible battle. Nevertheless, her decision is the inevitable one.

BOOK SEVEN: THE FINAL RESCUE

CHAPTER 1

Summary

Maggie returns to the mill on the fifth day after her departure. Tom has learned from Bob Jakin that Maggie was seen with Stephen at Mudport. He fully expects the worst—that she is not married. When Maggie comes to him for refuge, he angrily refuses to have her. He accuses her of using Philip as a screen to deceive Lucy, who is ill as a result and unable to speak to anyone. He will not shelter Maggie, for he wishes the world to know that *he* knows the difference between right and wrong.

Mrs. Tulliver is with Tom, and when she hears this she offers to go with Maggie. They go to Bob Jakin, who gives them lodging. Bob is perplexed that Maggie is not married, but for several days he asks no questions. Maggie at last asks him to bring Dr. Kenn to her, but Bob says that Mrs. Kenn has recently died, and the clergyman may not be going out. But talk-into to Maggie loosens Bob's tongue, and he offers to "leather" anyone who has offended Maggie. She declines the offer, saying that she has done wrong so often herself that she would not like to see anyone punished. This puzzles Bob, but he does not ask any other questions.

Commentary

Maggie's excuse to Tom is the same as she has always used: "I never meant to give way to my feelings." Tom is proved right in not having trusted her. Yet he appears at his worst here; his self-righteousness is loathsome. He says he will continue to provide for Maggie, but he has obviously forgotten the spirit of his father's injunction to care for her. He tells her, "I wash my hands of you for ever. You don't belong to me." Mr. Tulliver would never have acted so.

Bob Jakin's generosity again is a contrast. He has "the same chivalry towards dark-eyed Maggie, as in the days when he had bought her the memorable present of books." Bob is still the knight-errant who asks nothing for himself. Nevertheless, he is the one who puts the world's view of the situation: he is "sorely perplexed" as to how she and Stephen got away from each other; and he is unable to understand her feeling that "I shouldn't like to punish anyone, even if they'd done me wrong; I've done wrong myself too often." But although Bob's understanding of the matter is not much greater than anyone else's, he is far more sympathetic than the rest of the town is.

CHAPTER 2

Summary

It soon becomes known that Maggie has returned, and since she is unwed, all the blame falls on her. If she had returned as Stephen's wife, the affair would have been "quite romantic," and to refuse to associate with the couple would be nonsense. But since Maggie returned unwed, it was evident that her conduct "had been of the most aggravated kind." "Public opinion, in these cases, is always of the feminine gender—not the world, but the world's wife...." The world's wife assumes that Stephen refused to marry Maggie and recalls that Lucy and Philip have been treated badly. It is hoped that Maggie will leave "so as to purify the air of St. Ogg's...."

Maggie is filled with remorse and is unable to see either Philip or Lucy. She intends to take employment to support herself. She decides to carry her problems to Dr. Kenn. He is quietly kind and tells her that "the Church ought to represent the feeling of the community," but that Christian brotherhood hardly exists in the public. He says she probably does not anticipate the injustice she will receive; but she has begun to experience that already. A letter has arrived from Stephen, Dr. Kenn informs her. He has gone abroad and has written back to say that Maggie is blameless. However, the evidence is insufficient to satisfy public opinion. He advises her to "take a situation at a distance," but Maggie wishes to remain there. Dr. Kenn promises to try to find Maggie a position. After she leaves, he stands "ruminating." He has begun to feel that a marriage between Stephen and Maggie is "the least evil," but he appreciates that Maggie must regard it as "a desecration." He hesitates to intervene, for he realizes that life is too complex to be guided by general rules, and the special circumstance of Maggie's feeling would overturn a conclusion arrived at by "any balancing of consequences."

Commentary

"The world's wife" is the personification of public opinion. She appears to express the worst side of human nature, but the ironic treatment she receives makes her appear humorous as well as spiteful. Still, her conclusions are all the wrong ones; hers is an entirely superficial view. Maggie is considered to be "extremely dangerous to daughters [through] the taint of her presence." The world's wife is a quick and effective way for the author to put across the effect on St. Ogg's society of Maggie's escapade. She is a perfect vehicle for the author's comments on that society.

Young Torry once again epitomizes the masculine side of society's reaction to Maggie. He treats her "with the air of nonchalance which he might have bestowed on a friendly barmaid."

Maggie then realizes for the first time "that she would have other obloquy cast on her besides that which was felt to be due to her breach of faith towards Lucy." She has once again failed to see the consequences of her acts. She realizes her weakness, perhaps for the first time; but her main hope is for "something to guarantee her from more falling." This is one sign that she is still not fully ready to face life, for such a guarantee is impossible.

The reader is likely to feel, as does Dr. Kenn, that "an ultimate marriage between Stephen and Maggie [is] the least evil." Dr. Kenn sees as clearly as may be the difficulties in the case, but he has no very definite idea what to do. The author obviously intends this to be a difficult problem. "The great problem of the shifting relation between passion and duty is clear to no man who is capable of apprehending it." It is clear to the world's wife, but only because the world's wife cannot appreciate the difficulty. The same may be said of Tom. It has been demonstrated, as Dr. Kenn says, that "the persons who are the most incapable of a conscientious struggle such as yours, are precisely those who will be likely to shrink from you; because they will not believe in your struggle." And it is true that "the ideas of discipline and Christian fraternity are entirely relaxed — they can hardly be said to exist in the public mind" — that is, in the mind of "the world's wife." Dr. Kenn interprets for the reader the complexities of the problem and establishes a moral norm to set them against. Nevertheless, he is not a mere personification, such as the world's wife is. As will be seen later, he has human failings of his own.

CHAPTER 3

Summary

Aunt Glegg reproves Tom for "admitting the worst of his sister until he was compelled." Mr. Glegg, in his sympathy for Lucy, is set completely against Maggie; and Mrs. Pullet does not know how to act; but Mrs. Glegg stands firmly by her kin. She offers to take Maggie in and shelter her, although she still threatens to "give her good advice." Maggie is grateful, but she wishes to be independent.

There is word that Lucy is better, but nothing has been heard from Philip. At last Bob brings Maggie a letter from him. Philip writes that he believes in Maggie, that he was sure she meant to cleave to him and to renounce Stephen for his sake and for Lucy's. He believes that her love for Stephen comes from only part of her character, that there is something stronger in her than her love for Stephen. Philip could not bear to stand in her way, but only the thought that she might need him kept him from suicide. He says that she should have no self-reproaches because of him, for she has been true. He offers her any help he can give.

The letter makes Maggie sure that no happiness in love could make her forget the pain of others.

Commentary

The Dodson code fails when confronted with a thing "which had never happened before, so there was no knowing how to act." This is the same thing which confronted Mrs. Tulliver at the bankruptcy, but now it affects the whole clan. However, it does not affect them equally. Mrs. Glegg has sufficient strength of character to overcome it. It is "a case in which her hereditary rectitude and personal strength of character found a common channel along with her fundamental ideas of clanship." The other characters lack either her strength or her wholehearted devotion to the clan. She alone finds it necessary to stand by her kin "as long as there was a shred of honour attributable to them." Mrs. Glegg is perhaps the last person in whom this result would be expected; yet it seems natural when it happens.

In Tom, "family feeling had lost the character of clanship, in taking on a doubly deep dye of personal pride." This pride has been apparent from his boyhood, and now it reaches fruition in hate for his sister—"a repulsion towards Maggie that derived its very intensity from their early childish love." Because Maggie has been close to him, her waywardness is the stronger a blow to Tom's pride.

Mrs. Tulliver is becoming more of a person than she was before. She actually appears to have learned something from her misfortunes. "I must put up wi' my children...there's nothing else much to be fond on, for my furnitur' went long ago." She has at least a glimmering of understanding and thoughtfulness for others.

Philip, in his letter, shows a depth of understanding of Maggie's character that none of the other characters reach, not even Dr. Kenn. This letter presents his own sentiments with an intensity which has always been lacking before; for the first time there is no ambivalence in the author's attitude toward him; and he is all the more noble for the contrast of his emotional strength and his physical weakness. His letter establishes his final relationship to Maggie. Because of his love he is willing to sacrifice himself, not to avoid giving pain to another, but to give happiness. His is a sacrifice more positive than hers.

CHAPTER 4

Summary

Dr. Kenn has been unable to find any position for Maggie, and he finally decides that the only hope is for him to employ her himself. Most of his parishioners are set against her, and the few who are not are too timid to make their views public. Dr. Kenn takes Maggie on as governess to his children.

Dr. Kenn, "exemplary as he had hitherto appeared," now appears to have his weaknesses. It begins to be said that he may soon marry Maggie.

The Miss Guests, Stephen's sisters, know that Stephen wishes to marry Maggie, and their alarm that Maggie will relent prompts them to plan to take Lucy to the coast to meet Stephen as soon as Lucy can leave home. Lucy does not yet go out, and Maggie has no contact with her, although she hungers to see her. Maggie is sitting alone in her room one evening when Lucy appears. She has stolen out to see Maggie. Maggie tells her that she did not mean to deceive her, and that Stephen struggled too, that he will come back to her. Lucy cannot stay; but she promises to come to Maggie again when she returns from the coast, when she is stronger and can do as she pleases. Her parting words are that Maggie is better than she.

Commentary

The world's wife is dropped, but her place is taken by Society — the ladies' "favourite abstraction, called Society, which served to make their consciences perfectly easy in doing what satisfied their own egoism." The ladies, in the person of Society, are handled with the same irony as was the world's wife. Religion is seen to have no effect on their daily lives. Dr. Kenn has no more influence on Maggie's behalf than "if he had attempted to influence the shape of bonnets." The ladies have no problem maintaining views in opposition to his, for "they maintained them in opposition to a Higher Authority, which they had venerated longer." The author does not fail to relate their reaction to the reader's own in such cases: "they now thought her artful and proud; having quite as good grounds for that judgment as you and I probably have for many strong opinions of the same kind."

Lucy's innocence has always been emphasized, but she has always reacted in a human way. Now this places the author in a dilemma. It would be humanly natural for Lucy to wish to keep Stephen, but this would destroy her innocence, which Maggie cherishes. A more characteristic, and equally believable, reaction would be for her to give Stephen up, thus freeing Maggie; but this would destroy the story. Yet the author wishes to make the point that Maggie is a better person than Lucy. She covers over the problem by making their interview short and hurried, while still making the desired point.

CHAPTER 5

Summary

Rain has fallen continuously for two days, and the old men are re-minded of the weather which preceded the great floods of sixty years before. It is past midnight and raining heavily as Maggie sits alone in her room "battling with the old shadowy enemies." Two days earlier, Dr. Kenn was forced to release her from her position as governess because of the "gossip and slander" which had arisen. He has advised Maggie that it would be best for her to go away from St. Ogg's. Now Maggie has received a letter from Stephen, saying that two months have "deepened the certainty" that he can never care for life without her and asking her to write to him to come. Her longing for him and her misery combine to make her desire to write, and the thought that Stephen is miserable makes the desire stronger. But she recoils from that, and hours of prayer make her resolve to bear her burden. She burns the letter, vowing to "bear it till death," and wondering how soon death might come.

At that moment Maggie feels water about her knees. She starts up, knowing at once that it is the flood. She runs to wake Bob and hurries down to help him ready the boats. Maggie is swept away in one boat into the dark-ness. She floats out over the flooded fields, and in the growing twilight she sees St. Ogg's. She paddles to reach the mill, where the house stands "drowned up to the first story." Maggie calls, and Tom comes to the win-dow. Their mother is away at Garum Firs. Tom climbs out into the boat. When they are alone on the flood the meaning of this rescue comes to him in "a new revelation to his spirit, of the depths in life, that had lain be-yond his vision...." They set off to try to find Lucy, but below the wharves huge fragments are floating. People in a boat shout a warning, but Tom and Maggie are borne down by the drifting masses. They disappear "in an em-brace never to be parted."

Commentary

Dr. Kenn must face his own difficult moral problem. His answer, un-like Maggie's, is to succumb to necessity. "He was finally wrought upon by the consideration of the peculiar responsibility attached to his office, of avoiding the appearance of evil." This, it seems, he places above acting in accord with his conscience. The author never makes this central to Maggie's own situation, but it is certainly to be taken as a reflection on her choice of continued renunciation. A further comment on this is Dr. Kenn's belief that "conscientious people are apt to see their duty in that which is the most painful course." Certainly this is the case with Maggie.

Stephen's letter presents the greatest possible contrast with Philip's. Where the contrast of physical strength has been favorable to Stephen, here the moral contrast leaves no doubt as to Philip's superiority. Stephen's letter is entirely a statement of self-concern; it is the negation of the self-sacrifice which Maggie strives for.

The flood comes as the solution to Maggie's problems. The author has been preparing for this: there have been many hints and foreshadowings. But the flood is not a satisfactory solution, because it does not arise out of the situations or characters of the novel. Eliot has prepared for it, but not properly. It should be compared to the sudden end of the lawsuit with Pivart. That event was prepared briefly, but skillfully, and kept at the back of the reader's mind through frequent reminders. When it came, it seemed natural. Eliot tries to do the same with the flood but fails in this more important attempt. The reason is that the flood is completely external—it has no relation to Maggie or her problems—while the lawsuit was a result of Tulliver's character, and some occurrence of that sort could hardly have been avoided. While the lawsuit and its outcome were functional parts of the novel, the flood does not serve its purpose. Maggie has been brought into a final relationship of one sort or another with Philip and Lucy, but not with Stephen or Tom. The flood is used to bring about her final reconciliation with Tom, but it is not a satisfying one. And Stephen is merely passed off. Maggie's quick death is not poetic justice, but a quick way out. The results of her moral decision are never seen. The reunion with Tom is oversimplified. In contrast to the full treatment of their early lives, this section passes over things of the utmost importance. The author herself wrote, "I could not develop as fully as I wished the concluding 'Book' in which the tragedy occurs, and which I had looked forward to with much attention and premeditation from the beginning." The real failure is that the flood is an evasion of the moral problems raised, and that Maggie's life ends just as she is reaching a significant stage in her development. Tom's conversion too, this "new revelation to his spirit," comes too suddenly to be meaningful.

CONCLUSION

Summary

The fifth year after the flood, little trace of its desolation is visible. The autumn is "rich in golden corn-stacks"; the wharves and warehouses are busy again. But scars of the flood are still to be seen, and "uptorn trees are not rooted again." The mill has been rebuilt. In Dorlcote churchyard, near the grave of "a father whom we know," has been erected a tomb for two bodies found after the flood. The tomb has been visited by two men who felt that "their keenest joy and keenest sorrow were for ever buried there."

One of them came again years after "with a sweet face beside him." The other was always alone. On the tomb, below Tom and Maggie's names, is written, "In their death they were not divided."

Commentary

This section provides a neat wrap-up of the lives of the characters through its hints at the later lives of those who remain. Stephen and Lucy marry, while Philip remains true to the memory of Maggie. Tom and Maggie return at last to their childhood relationship in the permanent reconciliation of death.

CHARACTER ANALYSES

THE DODSON SISTERS

Mrs. Glegg, Mrs. Pullet, Mrs. Deane, and Mrs. Tulliver are recognizably members of the same family, even without their own constant reminders of that fact. All of them give allegiance to the same code for living, a code based on respect for property and strict maintenance of tradition. But each of the four has personal traits which mark her out from the others. With Mrs. Pullet it is her extreme care for personal possessions and her mild hypochrondria and interest in the diseases of other persons. Mrs. Tulliver has the same attitude toward her personal treasures coupled with greater-than-ordinary stupidity. Hers is a mind which runs on a single track. Mrs. Deane is less definitely characterized, but commands respect through the superior wealth and position of her husband. Mrs. Glegg is the one most interested in property, but she pays little attention to her personal goods. Her mind runs more to cash. She is by far the most strict in her observance of the traditional rites and customs. She sets the standards for the rest of the family, who follow as best they can. She is an arrogant woman, but not without virtues of her own. Her shrewdness is always put to good use; and she is the only one, in the end, to whom kinship remains more important than the opinions of society. If she represents the Dodson code at its worst—egoistic, grasping, and uncharitable—she epitomizes the best side as well.

The Dodson code is slightly exaggerated for comic effect. Yet all the sisters remain human; they are not caricatures. The code which underlies their actions presents a standard of human conduct. However erroneous it may seem at times, it nevertheless offers a consistent and believable reference point for the actions of that side of Maggie's family.

TOM TULLIVER

On his first appearance, he already presents most of the characteristics he will have as a man. That is not to say that Tom does not change: he changes greatly as he matures. But the man is readily visible in the boy.

As a boy Tom is already strict with his sister, and fully convinced that it is for her own good. He is equally convinced that he can do no wrong. He sets his own standards of conduct, and so long as he maintains them he feels no pangs of conscience. And he always maintains his own standards. The fact that these often give pain to others — chiefly Maggie — is no concern of his.

His father's bankruptcy is the central event in Tom's life. Before it, he is a boy. After it, he is a man. The change is abrupt, but it is thoroughly convincing, for only a slight shift in values, and a slight increase in self-confidence, is involved. Tom the man is the same person. He is unimaginative but very clear-sighted. He always considers the possible, and will not look beyond that. Where, as a boy, he had little use for Maggie's imaginative games, now he easily gives up his own dreams of "cutting a fine figure." When the means are removed, the dream goes also.

In some ways Tom seems to have inherited the worst of both sides of his family. He has the Dodson strictness and respect for property, but not the strong feeling of kinship. He has his father's hard-headedness, his belief in himself, and his tendency to remember grudges; but he has none of his father's warmth and generosity. He cannot comprehend the nature of his father's charge to "care for the little wench." He sees "care" in terms of money and property, as would his mother's family, rather than thinking of love and kindness.

Only at the very end, when it is already too late, does Tom come to see that he has overlooked a large part of life. But that recognition brings him to a momentary reunion with Maggie before they die together.

MAGGIE TULLIVER

She is in most ways the opposite of Tom. She is her father's daughter, and she has inherited his warm feeling for other people and his impetuosity. But she has none of his masculine self-assurance.

As a child Maggie is highly intelligent, but likely to be forgetful. She acts rashly without considering consequences. This is one of the results of her great sensitivity, for she cannot abide criticism or harsh judgments on her. By the same token, she never judges others harshly. She has none of Tom's arrogant self-righteousness. She is easily convinced that she has done wrong, despite the injury this causes to her sensitive soul. She is somewhat vain about her cleverness, but as this is never recognized by the people around her, it never turns into conceit.

For Maggie, as for Tom, the bankruptcy is one of the most important events of her life; but it affects her in a different way. While it is a goad to Tom's ambition, it drives Maggie to renunciation of the world which treats her so harshly. At first this takes the form of simple helping around home and giving up of childish self-indulgence; but the discovery of Thomas à Kempis gives method and meaning to her renunciation. Nevertheless hers remains basically a childish revolt, a hope of avoiding pain by giving up pleasure.

Maggie's concern for other people is the thing which breaks her free from this self-imposed exile. She begins to see Philip Wakem out of pity for him, and he reawakens her desire for life. This desire is one of the two most important threads in Maggie's character. It is a desire to have "more of everything," and it corresponds to the other characters' desire for property. Only Maggie and Philip show it in this form, as a longing for music, art, and life.

Maggie's wish to avoid hurting people finally comes in opposition to her desires. Her failure to resolve that conflict leads her to the point of having to choose whom she will hurt. She sees it as a conflict of duty and passion, but that is only part of the problem. In her case it becomes difficult to tell just where duty lies. At this crisis she reacts as she did to the bankruptcy: she banishes herself. Her reaction is consistent with what has been seen of her since childhood. It represents the fruit of the moral system she has been building for herself, a system based on the good of others. She carries it through with great determination, even when she finds that, as before, she has not foreseen many of the consequences.

STEPHEN GUEST

He is alone among the major characters in being essentially described, rather than *shown* to be what the author wishes him to be. By description he is handsome, witty, and a powerful personality. However, he appears as a bit of a fop, a fine young gentleman who will be of account through his father's fortune, if at all. Stephen suffers from having to be the chosen object of the love of the main character in the novel. He cannot be developed at the expense of that character, and consequently he tends to be underdone.

He never quite measures up to Maggie's love. Stephen loves Maggie against his will and his judgment. There can be no doubt of the reality of his love, but he has not the self-sacrificing nature of Maggie and Philip. By contrast with them he appears selfish. Yet he cannot be considered a cad, for his love brings him real suffering.

LUCY DEANE

She is in most ways a contrast to Maggie. As a child she is all the things Maggie is not: she is quiet, well-behaved, neat, and not over-intelligent. She is "pretty little pink-and-white Lucy," and this remains the basis of her adult character. However, as an adult Lucy takes on considerably more depth. Her reactions and her thoughts are secondary to Maggie's, and as a result they are played down. But she has human reactions and human complexity. Lucy's complexity can be easily overlooked because it is of such a subdued kind, especially in Maggie's presence.

PHILIP WAKEM

He is drawn in more intricate detail than are Stephen and Lucy; he is treated almost as fully as Maggie and Tom. He is perhaps more complex than either of those two. From the first Philip is seen to be talented, kind-hearted, and sensitive. He draws well without lessons; although Tom insults him, he has sympathy for Tom's injury and understands his fear of being crippled; he alone shares Maggie's intense desire for a full life. Indeed, in most ways he appears to be a good match for Maggie. Yet there is something always wrong with Philip. That something is not exactly his deformity, but it is connected with it. The real problem is that Philip is so completely unmanly. There can be no doubt that the author intends this effect; she frequently contrasts Philip's weakness to Stephen's strength and remarks on his feminine sensitiveness. It is this which makes Maggie's temporary love for Philip such an uneasy relationship.

Philip's virtues should not be overlooked. In the end he displays true nobility of character. He makes a sacrifice as great as Maggie's, although less dramatic. And his depth of understanding of other persons is unmatched in the novel: his remarks throw light on many of the other characters. Yet his virutes remain inseparable from his one great weakness.

DIRECT ADDRESS AND
AUTHORIAL COMMENT

The author makes extensive use of direct address to comment on the action or on characters, either in her own voice or in that of the narrator.

This is a technique which is little used in present-day fiction. It has been almost entirely supplanted by Henry James's concept of the novel as a separate self-contained world which makes no reference to author or reader. However, it was standard technique in Eliot's day for the author to address the reader.

Such comment is combined with an onmiscient point of view in order to help the reader better understand the characters and their problems. In this novel the author is aiming specifically at enlarging the reader's understanding of the complexities of human life. George Eliot once wrote, "The only effect I ardently long to produce by my writings is, that those who read them should be better able to *imagine* and to *feel* the pains and the joys of those who differ from themselves in everything but the broad fact of being struggling, erring, human creatures." Her technique is appropriate to this aim.

The author's comments are often an analysis of a character or of society. Consider Book I, Chapter 12: "the mind of St. Ogg's did not look extensively before or after. It inherited a long past without thinking of it, and had no eyes for the spirits that walked the streets.... The days were gone when people could be greatly wrought upon by their faith, still less change it: the Catholics were formidable because they would lay hold of government and property, and burn men alive; not because any sane and honest parishioner of St. Ogg's could be brought to believe in the Pope.... Dissent was an inheritance along with a superior pew and a business connection...." Such comment can produce an intimacy as deep as that given by internal representation of a character's thoughts. It also helps to place the character in a detailed social context. Eliot said it was her habit to "strive after as full a vision of the medium in which a character moves as of the character itself."

The author's comments help the reader to maintain the proper attitude to the characters. When Maggie is swept away by the writings of Thomas à Kempis, the author provides a mature analysis of her immature reaction: "She had not perceived — how could she until she had lived longer? — the inmost truth of the old monk's outpourings, that renunciation remains sorrow, though a sorrow borne willingly. Maggie was still panting for happiness, and was in ecstasy because she had found the key to it" (Book IV, Chapter 3).

Often the author speaks on behalf of characters who are inarticulate in themselves. Mrs. Tulliver is consistently explained to us, although usually in an ironic manner. Nevertheless, the author's attitude is one of sympathy, not satire. This is true even when she speaks for characters who are generally capable of expressing themselves. She continually strives to put the reader in sympathy with all the characters, to help him realize the complexity of all human relationships. Stephen may be taken as an example: "It is clear to you, I hope, that Stephen was not a hypocrite—capable of deliberate doubleness for a selfish end; and yet his fluctuations between the indulgence of a feeling and the systematic concealment of it, might have made a good case in support of Philip's accusation" (Book VI, Chapter 9).

The author often addresses the reader to add judgments of her own to the raw data of the story. That is, she presents the world after a process of thought and consideration. This being the case, the quality of the judgments becomes important. One of the fine points of the novel is the soundness of the author's observations on society and on people, on human emotions and relationships. Often enough these are commonplaces, but they are rarely commonplace. The author has a knack for making common truths satisfying. From Book IV, Chapter 2: "There is something sustaining in the very agitation that accompanies the first shocks of trouble, just as an acute pain is often a stimulus, and produces an excitement which is transient strength. It is in the slow, changed life that follows—in the time when sorrow has become stale, and has no longer an emotive intensity that counteracts its pain—in the time when day follows day in dull unexpectant sameness, and trial is a dreary routine;—it is then that despair threatens; it is then that the peremptory hunger of the soul is felt, and eye and ear are strained after some unlearned secret of our existence, which shall give to endurance the nature of satisfaction."

Frequently the comments are used as technical points—to shift the point of view, to underline character or action, to give the effect of passage of time. More than once they provide a key to the imagery being used. But normally they are meant to involve the reader, to connect the world of the novel with his own. For this reason they should not engage him in debate or distract him. On occasion they fail, but the occasions are rare. The failures are due to archness, aggressiveness, or florid rhetoric. Chapter 12 of Book I contains a case which falls flat through straining after humor: "...the black ships unlade themselves of their burthens from the far north, and carry away, in exchange, the precious inland products, the well-crushed cheese and the soft fleeces, which my refined readers have doubtless become acquainted with through the medium of the best classic pastorals." However, for the most part the comments are delightful in themselves. They contain much of the humor of the book. The author shows a sure comic touch in such lines as: "Such glances and tones bring the breath of poetry with them into a room that is half-stifling with glaring gas and hard flirtation"; or,"They didn't know there was any other religion, except that of chapel-goers, which appeared to run in families, like asthma." Like these, the comments are generally ironic and often witty. They should not be seen as blemishes in the novel, but as an integral and important part of the author's technique.

QUESTIONS FOR REVIEW

1. Would the author agree that Maggie dies just as she is reaching a crucial stage in her development?

2. In what ways does the author use irony, and what is her purpose in using it?

3. Compare the decision which Maggie makes in giving up Stephen to Dr. Kenn's decision to send her away. What is the moral basis of each decision? How does one reflect upon the other?

4. What sort of commitments does Maggie feel she has broken when she elopes with Stephen? Would the other characters feel as she does about these commitments? What factors in her early life might lead Maggie to hold these views?

5. Distinguish those characters in the novel who exist functionally—that is, to state a point of view—from those whose existence is an end in itself.

6. Is Maggie idealized because of George Eliot's emotional involvement with her?

7. D. H. Lawrence considered Eliot to be the first novelist to start "putting all the action inside." Apply this to *The Mill on the Floss.*

8. How does the novel illustrate that character is "not the whole of our destiny?"

9. Contrast Aunt Moss's home life with that of Mrs. Glegg and Mrs. Pullet.

10. Comment on George Eliot's dramatic sense or her descriptive powers or her ability as a philosopher.

11. What purposes does imagery serve in *The Mill on the Floss?*

12. "It is the habit of my imagination to strive after as full a vision of the medium in which a character moves as of the character itself." Does Eliot succeed in this?

13. It has been said that Eliot's work has "Tolstoyan depth and reality without Tolstoyan range." How well does this apply to *The Mill on the Floss?*

SELECTED BIBLIOGRAPHY

Bennett, Joan. *George Eliot, Her Mind and Her Art.* London: Cambridge University Press, 1948.

Cecil, David. *Victorian Novelists.* Chicago: University of Chicago Press, 1958. (Paperback)

Hardy, Barbara. *The Novels of George Eliot.* London: The Athlone Press, 1959.

Harvey, W. J. *The Art of George Eliot.* New York: Oxford University Press, 1962.

Leavis, F. R. *The Great Tradition.* London: Chatto and Windus, 1948.

Thale, Jerome. *The Novels of George Eliot.* New York: Columbia University Press, 1959.

NOTES